EASY KATAKANA

How to Read and Write English Words Used in Japanese

Tina Wells

Editorial Consultant
Aoi Yokouchi

PASSPORT BOOKS
a division of *NTC Publishing Group*
Lincolnwood, Illinois USA

Also available
Easy Hiragana

Cover design by Fujihiko Kaneda

1995 Printing

This edition first published in 1989 by Passport Books,
a division of NTC Publishing Group,
4255 West Touhy Avenue, Lincolnwood (Chicago), Illinois 60646-1975 U.S.A.
Originally published by Yohan Publications, Inc. ©Yohan Publications, Inc.

8 9 10 11 VRS/VRS 0 4

TABLE OF CONTENTS

About the Author

TINA WELLS, author of *Speaking for Communication* (ICI, Tokyo) and co-author of *Spelling Mastery Series* (SRA, Chicago). She is a Phi Beta Kappa graduate in Linguistics from the University of Oregon. AOI YOKOUCHI, her sensei in Japanese, provided invaluable insights and assistance from start to finish.

INTRODUCTION

What is *Easy Katakana*? It is 20 easy lessons for perfecting loanword literacy. What are loanwords? They are words coming from outside Japan, in Japanese these words are called "gairaigo". Katakana is the spelling system used to spell gairaigo.

Gairaigo is a very important part of the Japanese language, up to 80 percent of the language used in Japanese advertising is gairaigo. Japanese people often wrongly assume Westerners can understand gairaigo. Japanese language texts traditionally avoid teaching gairaigo and place little or no emphasis on teaching katakana. Westerners, however, find gairaigo extremely useful in day-to-day survival in Japan.

Katakana literacy will enable you to read familiar food names on menus (coffee, hamburger, salad), to read key words on signs (elevator, taxi, toilet, curb), and operate some equipment (start, stop, clear). Learning gairaigo will enhance your Japanese vocabulary with easy-to-remember, descriptive words (gorgeous, grotesque, sexy). Writing katakana will enable you to spell your name in Japanese.

Although most gairaigo originate from familiar Western words, they are not always easy to recognize, even if you can read katakana. The main reason is that familiar words are transformed by the Japanese sound system into unfamiliar-sounding words, for example: coffee is kōhii, credit card is kurejitto kādo, London is rondon, and Cynthia is shinshia.

Most of the sound changes are predictable, you will see this as the program progresses. Even after you understand the sound changes, though, there is no predicting which words will become shortened: suto from strike, wāpuro from word processor, rimokon from remote control.

Another obstacle for decoding gairaigo is Japanese-English. This form of gairaigo takes familiar English words and assigns new meanings to them: torampu (trump) refers to card-playing, never a trump card; rezā (leather) refers to *imitation* leather. Compound words are even more interesting: petto hoteru (pet + hotel = kennel); kanningu pēpā (cunning + paper = cheat sheet); pēpā doraibā (paper + driver = driver with a license but no car).

This book is designed to teach you to read starting from Day 1. Traditional katakana books force the learner to learn dozens of symbols before learning to read a single word. The words then introduced are rarely useful and rarely defined. It is understandable why many learners quickly lose interest and never become completely literate.

HOW TO USE THIS BOOK

The first 19 lessons in *Easy Katakana* are divided into six sections: New Kana, Recognition, Key Words, Practice, New Words, and Challenge.

At the beginning of every lesson is a katakana chart completed to date. Katakana symbols introduced in that lesson appear in boldface type in the chart. A completed katakana chart like that from Lesson 20 follows for your reference. (Appendix A gives corresponding sounds and lessons on which each kana is taught.)

ア	カ	サ	タ	ナ	ハ	マ	ヤ	ラ	ワ
イ	キ	シ	チ	ニ	ヒ	ミ	(ヰ)	リ	ン
ウ	ク	ス	ツ	ヌ	フ	ム	ユ	ル	
エ	ケ	セ	テ	ネ	ヘ	メ	(ヱ)	レ	
オ	コ	ソ	ト	ノ	ホ	モ	ヨ	ロ	

You will study how to read and write approximately four or five new kana symbols or kana combinations in each lesson. These appear in the New Kana section. Boxes are provided so you can practice writing the new kana. Writing the new kana will make reading them easier. (If you would like more practice writing, use separate boxed or graph paper.)

The Recognition section tests your recognition of individual kana before going on to grouped kana (words). Kana in this section are listed in Japanese alphabetical order. Fill in the appropriate roman spelling for each kana in the blank provided. To check your answers, refer to Appendix A in the back of the book.

Learning just individual kana symbols will not make you a fluent reader. The Key Words section will give you a chance to read and write real katakana words, gairaigo. (Again, if you want more writing practice, use a separate sheet of paper.) The information accompanying the Key Words will help you understand pronunciation patterns, spelling conventions, word definitions, and/or word histories.

Following the Key Words section is a Practice section designed to test your whole-word recognition skills. Answers for this section appear at the end of each lesson. Any word missed should be written at least once as practice on a separate sheet of paper.

The New Words section can be used for reading practice, writing practice, and/or vocabulary building, whatever you wish. Since there are over 1,500 words in the New Words sections, you may wish to reserve writing practice only for those words you have trouble decoding. For decoding practice: cover up the roman spelling, sound out the katakana symbols, uncover the roman spelling and check your pronunciation against it. Guessing the Japanese definitions of gairaigo can be fun. Try this on your own or with friends after sounding out individual words.

A subsection of New Words entitled People starts on Lesson 2. Another subsection, Places, starts on Lesson 3. Decoding a word in either of these categories and guessing its English equivalent is easier because you know the word is limited to being either a person's name, or a place.

The final section is the Challenge section. These tasks are intended to be fun, but not too easy. Their answers follow at the end of each lesson.

Lesson 20 has a slightly different format from the other lessons. In this lesson the Japanese-English alphabet is taught and skills from throughout the program, such as alphabetizing Japanese-style, are tested and reviewed.

Don't overlook the appendices at the end of the book. Appendices A-D summarize pronunciation and spelling conventions.

One last note, not all gairaigo spellings have been standardized. This is especially true with names. Don't be surprised if three different people spell your name three different, but similar, ways. Choose or create a spelling you think comes closest to the sounds in your name, and use it.

Good luck!

EASY KATAKANA

LESSON 1

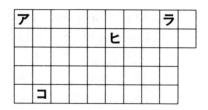

NEW KANAS

An alphabet that is made up entirely of syllables is called a syllabary. Japanese has two syllabaries, hiragana and katakana. The katakana syllabary is used to spell words borrowed from English, Dutch, French, etc.

Each katakana character (kana) represents one short syllable. Study how to pronounce the following kana. Next, practice writing them using the same strokes as in the examples.

コ = ko, similar to the ko's in kosher and Koran, but shorter.

ヒ = hi, similar to the hi in Tahiti.

ア = a, as in ah!, but shorter.

ラ = ra, similar to the ra in rah, but the tongue flaps against the roof of the mouth making it sound almost like dah or lah. It never sounds like rrrrrah!

A bar after a katakana symbol (like that over ā, ē, ō, or ū in roman spelling) doubles the time the vowel is held (ア = ah, ア— = aah).

kō 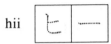   ā   rā

A doubled i is usually written ii in roman spelling because it is easier to read than ī.

hii

RECOGNITION

Write the roman spellings for each of the following kana.

ア _a_   コ ___   コ—___   ヒ—___   ラ—___

<ra hii ǎ ko kō >

KEY WORDS

Study the following key words, then practice writing them.

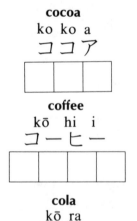

cocoa
ko ko a
コ コ ア

This is pronounced with an ah-sound at the end: ko-ko-a, not koh-koh. There are 5 letters in the English spelling of cocoa, but only 3 kanas in the katakana spelling.

coffee
kō hi i
コ — ヒ —

This is pronounced kōhii. The sound /fi/ is not native to Japanese. When this word was borrowed from the Dutch, /hii/ was substituted for /fii/.

cola
kō ra
コ — ラ

There is no true l-sound in Japanese, so cola is written kōra, with r. This r, how-ever, sounds like a cross between English r, l, and d.

4

PRACTICE

Japanese can be written vertically as well as horizontally. Look at the following menu items. How much is a coffee? A cola? Hot cocoa?

コーヒー ¥550	コーラ ¥450	ココア ¥500

NEW WORDS (including Key Words)

Practice reading and writing the following words.

コアラ [koara] = a koala bear.

コーヒー [kōhii] = coffee; from Dutch koffie.

ココア [kokoa] = cocoa, hot chocolate; from the written English word cocoa.

コーラ [kōra] = a cola drink.

コーラ [kōra] = Cora, a woman's name.

CHALLENGE

Which word do you think came into Japanese first: cocoa, cola or coffee?

ANSWERS

Recognition: a, ko, kō, hii, ra.

Practice: coffee ¥550, cola ¥450, hot cocoa ¥500.

Challenge: Coffee, brought by the Dutch in the 1600's, came first.

LESSON 2

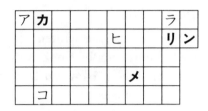

NEW KANAS

Study how to pronounce the following kana and practice writing them.

カ = ka, similar to the ca in calm, *not* like the ca's in Canada and America.

メ = me, similar to the me in nutmeg.

リ = ri, similar to both the de and ry in deary.

ン = n, similar to the n in income and the ng's in Hong Kong.
Unlike most kana it has a long *upward* stroke.

ン ン ン ン

RECOGNITION

The first kana in the syllabary is ア, a. The last kana is ン, n. The following kana are listed in Japanese alphabetical order. Write the roman spellings for each of them.

6

ア＿ カ＿ コ＿ ヒ *hi* メ＿ ラ＿ リ＿ ン＿

<*a hi ka ko me n ra ri*>

KEY WORDS

Study the following key words, then practice writing them.

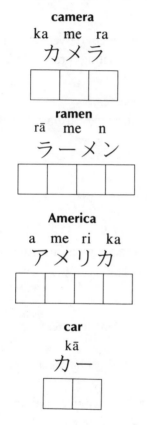

camera
ka me ra
カメラ

This is pronounced ka-me-ra, not *kam-ruh*. Names of most (but not all) modern inventions are written in katakana.

ramen
rā me n
ラーメン

Sometimes words coming from Chinese are written in katakana. Ramen noodles originated in China. All Japanese words end either with a vowel sound or an n, ン.

America
a me ri ka
アメリカ

There are no capital letters to learn in katakana. This is pronounced a-me-ri-ka, not uh-*me*-ri-kuh. There are no uh-sounds in Japanese. アメリカ means the United States of America.

car
kā
カー

Some English speakers pronounced car ka-uh; in Japanese this becomes ka-a. This word is not used by itself, only in compounds like: supōtsu kā, a sports car; kā mēkā, a car maker; and ria kā, "rear car". リアカー (ria kā) is an original Japanese word for a small, two-wheeled trailer-cart.

PRACTICE

All of the following words have ah-sounds in Japanese, but uh- or er-sounds in English. Draw lines to match these words.

7

アメリカ ●	● car maker
カメラ ●	● camera
コカコーラ ●	● curler
カーメーカー ●	● America
カーラー ●	● "rear car"
リアカー ●	● Coca-Cola

NEW WORDS (including Key Words)

Use the following words for reading practice (cover up the roman spelling, read, then check), and for writing practice (use a separate sheet of boxed or graph paper).

アメリカ [amerika] = the United States of America.

アメリカンコーヒー [amerikan kōhii] = weak coffee; from "American" + "coffee".

アリア [aria] = an aria (Western music).

カー [kā] = car; used only in compounds.

カーメーカー [kā mēkā] = car manufacturer, car maker.

カメラ [kamera] = a camera.

カラー [karā] = 1) color; only in compounds like karā purinto, color print, and karā terebi, color television. 2) a collar, usually Western-style.

カーラー [kārā] = a curler, curling iron.

コカコーラ [kokakōra] = Coca-Cola.

コーン [kōn] = 1) cone, as in aisu kuriimu kōn, ice cream cone. 2) corn, maize.

コリー [korii] = a collie; all Western breeds of dogs have katakana names.

メーカー [mēkā] = manufacturer, maker; usually used in compounds.

メカ [meka] = a mechanism; abbreviated from mekanizumu.

メーン [mēn] = the state of Maine.

ラーメン [rāmen] = ramen noodles, ramen soup; from Chinese la-mien.

リアカー [ria kā] = a small trailer with two large tires pulled by a person or a bicycle; from "rear" + "sidecar".

8

PEOPLE

アンリ [anri] = Henri (from French)
アラン [aran] = Alan
ヒラリー [hirarii] = Hilary
メーラ [mērā] = Mailer
メリー [merii] = Mary
ラリー [rarii] = Larry
リー [rii] = Lee
リン [rin] = Lynn
リリアン [ririan] = Lilian

CHALLENGE

1. Sometimes a dot (·) is written to represent an original hyphen. Where would the dot go in コカコーラ ?
2. Melancholy has been adopted into Japanese. It is a popular, not clinical, word. How do you think it is spelled in katakana?
3. The two r's in spo*r*ts ca*r* are both written with a dash in katakana but are not pronounced the same way. How do you suppose they are pronounced?

ANSWERS

Practice:

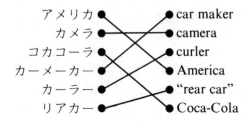

Challenge:
1. Between koka and kōra: コカ · コーラ.
2. melancholy = メランコリー [merankorii]
3. The dash in kā (car) prolongs the a-sound. The dash in supōtsu (sports) is like the dash in kōn (corn), it prolongs the o-sound.

LESSON 3

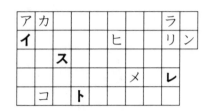

NEW KANAS

Study how to pronounce the following kana and practice writing them.

> レ = re, similar to the re in red, but not unlike the dea in dead and the le in led.

> ト = to, similar to the to's in tone and torn, but shorter.

> イ = i, similar to the i's in tuttifrutti.

> ス = su as in Sudan, or often just s (before a t, k, h or p, or at the end of a phrase), transcribed *su* or s'.

RECOGNITION

The following kana are listed in Japanese alphabetical order. Write the roman spellings for each of them.

ア＿ イ＿ カ＿ コ＿ ス＿ ト＿

ヒ_ メ_ ラ_ リ_ レ_ ン_

<a hi i ka ko me n ra re ri su to>

KEY WORDS

Study the following key words, then practice writing them.

curried rice
ka rē
カレー

ra i su
ライス

restaurant
re su to ra n
レストラン

toilet
to i re
トイレ

raincoat
re i n
レイン

kō to
コート

Because katakanized words can become very long, parts are often dropped. In this word -ed has been lost. This is usually written as one word with no separation between karē and rais*u*. The final u in rais*u* is often whispered: rais*u*=rais'.

The absence of a final t relects the original French pronunciation. The combination su+to is regularly pronounced *su*to: res*u*toran=res'toran. A レストラン serves Western-style food, not traditional Japanese specialties.

Toire is an abbreviation of toiretto. Both these words refer to the room, never the fixture. They are also euphemisms, they sound nicer than native Japanese equivalents.

Many final t-sounds become ト, as in reinkō*to* and toiret*to*. Some words with a long eh-sound can be written two ways, for example raincoat can also be written with a ― instead of イ: レーンコ ―ト. Although these words are spelled differently, they have the same pronunciation: reinkōto=rēnkōto.

11

PRACTICE

All of the following words have ス. When followed by a t, k, h, p or silence, ス is pronounced /s'/. If followed by anything else, ス is pronounced /su/.

Match these katakana words to their pronunciations. Then match the pronunciations to their English equivalents:

レストラン ●	● s'koa ●	● restaurant
レスラー ●	● resurā ●	● wrestler
スコア ●	● s'kāto ●	● iced coffee
アイスコーヒー ●	● res'toran ●	● Swiss
スイス ●	● ais'kōhii ●	● score
スカート ●	● suis' ●	● skirt

NEW WORDS (including Key Words)

アイアン [aian] = metal-headed "iron" golf club.

アイスコーヒー [aisu kōhii] = iced coffee.

アイスココア [aisu kokoa] = cold or "iced" cocoa, chocolate milk.

アントレ [antore] = an entree; from French.

イラスト [irasuto] = an illustration; shortened from irasutorēshon.

カレー [karē] = curry; from the Tamil word for curry, kari.

カレーライス [karē raisu] = curried rice, usually mildly curried beef
  stew on rice.

コイン [koin] = a general word for coins.

コーラス [kōrasu] = a chorus.

コレラ [korera] = cholera.

コート [kōto] = 1) a light-weight coat. 2) a court, as in tenisu kōto,
  tennis court.

メーンコース or メインコース [mēn kōsu] = a main course.

メンス [mensu] = a euphemism for menstruation.

ライス [raisu] = rice served Western-style with a fork or spoon.

ライスカレー [raisu karē] = less common equivalent for karēraisu.

レインコート or レーンコート [rēnkōto] = a raincoat.

12

レース [rēsu] = 1) lace. 2) a race.

レスラー [resurā] = a professional Western-style wrestler.

レストラン [resutoran] = a restaurant that serves Western-style food; from French.

リースカー [riisu kā] = a leased car.

リンス [rinsu] = (hair) rinse.

リレー [rirē] = a relay or a relay race.

スイートコーン [suiito kōn] = sweet corn, corn.

スカート [sukāto] = a skirt.

スコア [sukoa] = a score in sports or games.

スライス [suraisu] = sliced, in compounds like suraisu hamu, sliced ham.

スト [suto] = a walkout, a strike; radically shortened from suto-raiki, "strike".

ストア [sutoa] = store, shop; used mainly in names, as in Tōkyu sutoa, The Tokyu Store.

ストレス [sutoresu] = mental stress.

ストレート [sutorēto] = 1) straight in the sense of undiluted, un-mixed. 2) a straight line, victory, etc. in sports.

トイレ [toire] = a restroom, room with a toilet; shortened from toiretto.

トランス [toransu] = a transformer.

トレー [torē] = a tray in a copying machine or self-service restaurant (not a traditional Japanese serving tray).

トリートメント [toriitomento] = commercial remedy or treatment.

トースト [tōsuto] = a piece of toast.

PLACES

アラスカ [arasuka] = Alaska
イラン [iran] = Iran
メーン or メイン [mēn] = Maine
スイス [suisu] = Switzerland, Swiss
スリランカ [suri ranka] = Sri Lanka

PEOPLE

アレン [aren] = Allen
イアン [ian] = Ian
カレン [karen] = Karen
ライアン [raian] = Ryan

レイ [rei] = Ray
レスリー [resurii] = Leslie
リスト [risuto] = Liszt
スー [sū] = Sue

CHALLENGE

1. What do these words have in common when written in katakana?
   Iced coffee, curried rice, leased car, sliced.
2. Two-part words are sometimes not separated at all, separated by
   a space, or separated by a dot. Fill in one separating dot for each
   of the following words. a) スイートコーン   b) スリランカ
   c) アイスコーヒー
3. There are two ways to spell the sound /rē/ and two ways to spell
   the sound /mē/. What are they?
4. Can you guess the English equivalents for these words?
   a) イースト b) スリラー   Clues: a) It begins with "ye" in
   English, but there are no longer any yi-sounds in Japanese.
   b) This can describe a movie or a book. It begins with "th" in
   English but there are no th-sounds in Japanese.

ANSWERS

Practice:

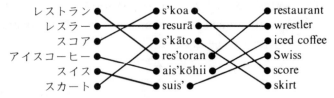

Challenge:

1. They all lose their -ed endings in katakana.
2. a) スイート・コーン (sweet corn) b) スリ・ランカ (Sri Lanka)
   c) アイス・コーヒー (iced coffee)
3. rē = レー or レイ. mē = メー or メイ.
4. a) イースト = yeast (iisuto) b) スリラー = thriller (surirā)

14

LESSON 4

ア	カ		タ				ラ	
イ		シ			ヒ		リ	ン
	ク	ス						
エ						メ	レ	
	コ		ト					

NEW KANAS

Study how to pronounce the following kana and practice writing them.

ク = ku, similar to the ku in Kuwait, but often k*u* (k'). The u is usually whispered when a t, s, h or p follows, or when it occurs at the end of a phrase.

タ = ta, similar to the ta in Taj Mahal. The first two strokes are the same as for ku.

エ = e, similar to the e in egg.

シ = shi, similar to the shi in shield, but the sh-sound is softer than in English. シ, shi, and ン, n, are the only kanas with a long final upward stroke.

15

RECOGNITION

The following kana are listed in Japanese alphabetical order. Write the roman spellings for each of them.

ア＿　イ＿　エ＿　カ＿　ク＿　コ＿　シ＿　ス＿

タ＿　ト＿　ヒ＿　メ＿　ラ＿　リ＿　レ＿　ン＿

<a e hi i ka ko ku me n ra re ri shi su ta to>

シ is not pronounced si, but some roman spelling systems spell it si.

KEY WORDS

Study the following key words, then practice writing them.

Yen
e n
エ ン

Yen became an English word when it was still being pronounced yen. The sound /ye/ is no longer used in Japanese, so yen is pronounced en. Advertisers sometimes spell Japanese words, like en, in katakana to attract attention.

cooler
kū rā
ク ー ラ ー

In Japanese this means an air conditioner which cools only a small area, like a room or car. It is not used to mean an ice chest except in the word aisukūrā, アイスクー ラー, a small bucket for ice cubes.

taxi
ta ku shi i
タ ク シ ー

The sound /si/ is not native to Japanese so the closest native syllable, shi, is usually substituted. The /u/ in the combination ku+s is regularly whispered, giving us tak'shii, rather than takushii.

escalator

e s*u* ka rē

エスカレ

tā

ー タ ー

Knowing the kanas for e, re, and tā will enable you to recognize the signs for elevators (er*e*bē *tā*) as well as the signs for escalators (エスカレーター). Any Japanese word can be broken after any kana and continued on the next line, and there is no special punctuation like a hyphen.

PRACTICE

The following modern devices all end with -tā in Japanese. Match them.

タクシーメーター ●   ● toaster
ライター ●   ● car heater
エスカレーター ●   ● lighter
トースター ●   ● escalator
スクーター ●   ● taximeter
カーヒーター ●   ● scooter

NEW WORDS (including Key Words)

アイスクーラー [ais*u* kūrā] = a small bucket for ice cubes; from "ice" + "cooler".

アシスタント [ashis*u*tanto] = a modern word for an assistant used especially in job titles.

エアコン [ea kon] = an air conditioning system which heats as well as cools; shortened from ea kondishonā.

エクレア [ekurea] = an eclair pastry.

17

エン [en] = yen; occasionally written in katakana for effect.

エンスト [ens*uto*] = an engine breakdown; from "engine" + "stop" or "stall" or "strike".

エラー [erā] = an error, especially in sports.

エレクトーン [erek*utō*n] = a Japanese-made word for an electric organ; from "electric" + "tone".

エリートコース [eriito kōs*u*] = getting a prestigeous position after graduating from a prestigeous university; from "elite" + "course".

エース [ēs*u*] = an ace in cards or sports.

エスカレーター [es*u*karētā] = an escalator.

インク [ink*u*] = fountain pen ink.

インスタントカレー [ins*u*tanto karē] = instant curry.

インスタントコーヒー [ins*u*tanto kōhii] = instant coffee.

インスタントラーメン [ins*u*tanto rāmen] = instant ramen.

イラストレーター [iras*u*torētā] = an illustrator.

カーヒーター [kāhiitā] = a car heater or heating system.

カークーラー [kākūrā] = a car cooler or cooling system.

コンクリート [konkuriito] = concrete.

クーラー [kūrā] = a small air conditioner for a room or car; also rūmukūrā ("room" + "cooler") or kākūrā.

クラス [kuras*u*] = a class in the sense of a group lesson.

クレーター [kurētā] = a crater on the moon.

クリア [kuria] = 1) clear color (as in nail enamel). 2) used on copying machines and such to mark the button that clears the counter.

メーター [mētā] = 1) a meter, as in gasumētā, a gas meter. 2) one of two spellings for metre, the unit of measure equal to 100cm.

ライター [raitā] = cigarette lighter.

レンタカー [rentakā] = a rent-a-car dealership or car.

レシート [reshiito] = a new word for a small, cash register receipt.

レタス [retas*u*] = lettuce.

シーン [shiin] = a scene in a movie.

シート [shiito] = 1) seat in a bus or train. 2) sheet of stamps or metal.

スクーター [sukūtā] = one of several words for a scooter or small motorbike.

スター [sutā] = a movie star.

スタイリスト [sutairisto] = a stylist.

スタート [sutāto] = starting line in sports or start button on some machines.

タイ [tai] = a necktie; from nekutai.

タクシー [takushii] = a taxi, taxicab.

タクシーメーター [takushiimētā] = a taximeter.

タンク [tanku] = tank for gas, oil, water, etc.

タレント [tarento] = T.V. talent, model, singer, etc.

トランク [toranku] = 1) trunk (boot) of a car. 2) trunk in the sense of a large carrying case.

トースター [tōsutā] = toaster, toaster oven.

PLACES

アトランタ [atoranta] = Atlanta
イエメン [iemen] = Yemen
イラク [iraku] = Iraq
イタリア [itaria] or イタリー [itarii] = Italy (from Italian "Italia" or English "Italy")
コスタリカ [kosuta rika] = Costa Rica
シリア [shiria] = Syria
シスコ [shisuko] = San Francisco (short for sanfuranshisuko)
タイ [tai] = Thailand, Thai

PEOPLE

エリー [erii] = Elly
エリントン [erinton] = Ellington (the g is ignored)
イエス [iesu] = Jesus (from Portuguese where J = /y/)
カーター [kātā] = Carter
クラーク [kurāku] = Clark
リタ [rita] = Rita
シーラ [shiira] = Sheila

シンクレア [shinkurea] ＝Sinclair
シンシア [shinshia] ＝Cynthia (cy and thi are both represented by shi)
スタンリー [sutanrii] ＝Stanley

CHALLENGE

1. The Japanese transliteration of Cynthia is シンシア. How do you think silicone and think tank are transliterated?
2. If operating a Japanese copying machine, could you recognize the start button and clear button? Write start and clear in katakana.
3. The word kusuri means medicine in Japanese. This word often appears outside pharmacies written in katakana to attract attention. How would you spell kusuri in katakana?
4. These organizations contain the letter C in English and in Japanese. What are they? a) シーアイエー b) イーイーシー

ANSWERS
Practice:

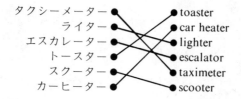

タクシーメーター● ●toaster
ライター● ●car heater
エスカレーター● ●lighter
トースター● ●escalator
スクーター● ●taximeter
カーヒーター● ●scooter

Challenge:

1. a) silicone＝シリコーン (shirikōn) b) think tank＝シンクタンク (shinku tanku)
2. start＝スタート; clear＝クリア
3. kusuri＝クスリ
4. a) the CIA (shii ai ē). b) the EEC (ii ii shii). The complete Japanese-English alphabet appears in Lesson 20.

20

LESSON 5

ア	カ		タ					ラ	
イ		シ			ヒ			リ	ン
	ク	ス	ツ			ム			
エ			テ			メ		レ	
オ	コ		ト						

NEW KANAS

Study how to pronounce the following kana and practice writing them.

オ = o, similar to the o's in Ohio and orient, but shorter.

二	寸	オ	オ	オ	オ					

テ = te, similar to the te in steak. Try not to confuse it with ラ, ra.

二	三	テ	テ	テ	テ					

ム = mu, a little shorter than the mu's in muumuu.

丛	ム	ム	ム	ム					

ツ = tsu, often ts*u* (ts'). This is pronounced as one syllable. At the ends of words and before s, k, p, h, it sounds like the ts in its, otherwise it resembles the tssu in "It's Sue". シ, shi, and ン, n, have final upward strokes, tsu does not.

ヽ	゛	ツ	ツ	ツ	ツ					

RECOGNITION

The following kana are listed in Japanese alphabetical order. Write the roman spellings for each of them.

21

ア＿　イ＿　エ＿　オ＿　カ＿　ク＿　コ＿
シ＿　ス＿　タ＿　ツ＿　テ＿　ト＿　ヒ＿
ム＿　メ＿　ラ＿　リ＿　レ＿　ン＿

⟨ *a e hi i ka ko ku me mu n o ra re ri* ⟩
shi su ta te to tsu

ツ is never pronounced tu, but some roman spelling systems spell it tu.

KEY WORDS

Study the following key words, then practice writing them.

twin

tsu i n

ツ イ ン

There are no /tu/ or /tw/ syllables in Japanese. Tsuin is the closest Japanese can come to twin. This word means either a twin bed or a hotel room with twin beds. In tsuin tawā, "twin towers", it means two-of-a-kind.

"cutlet(s)"

ka tsu re ts*u*

カ ツ レ ツ

In some words ツ is used instead of ト to represent t-sounds. Originally a katsurets*u* (or kats*u* for short) was a breaded and deep-fried cutlet. Now almost any meat breaded and deep-fried is called a カツ.

"omelet-rice"

o mu ra i s*u*

オ ム ラ イ ス

An omelet is called an omurets*u* (オ ム レ ツ) in Japanese. Omuraisu is an original Japanese creation of an omelet with a tomato sauce and rice filling usually topped with ketchup.

stereo

s*u* te re o

ス テ レ オ

This is pronounced s'tereo and means either a stereo set or stereophonic. This is not pronounced ste*rio*; the Japanese spelling is based on the English spelling, not the English pronunciation.

PRACTICE

Match the following "Western" foods.

オムレツ ●	● ice cream
ヒレカツ ●	● mousse
ムース ●	● omelet
アイスクリーム ●	● lime
カステラ ●	● "filet cutlet"
ライム ●	● "castella" sponge cake

NEW WORDS (including Key Words)

アイスクリーム [aisukuriimu] = ice cream.

ヒレ [hire] = filet; from French (compare the use of hi in both coffee and filet).

ヒレカツ [hire katsu] = a filet *katsuretsu*.

インテリ [interi] = an intelligent person.

インテリア [interia] = interior (design).

カメオ [kameo] = a cameo (jewelry).

カステラ [kasutera] = a sponge cake; from Portuguese pão de Castella, "bread from Castella".

カーステレオ [kā sutereo] = a car stereo.

カーテン [kāten] = curtain(s).

カツ or カツレツ [katsuretsu] = something (often a cutlet) deep-fried in breadcrumbs, not in tempura batter; from "cutlet".

コンテスト [kontesuto] = (beauty, singing or speech) contest.

クレムリン [kuremurin] = the Kremlin.

クリーム [kuriimu] = cream; in compounds like sawā kuriimu, sour cream, and kuriimu rinsu, cream rinse.

ムース [mūsu] = mousse.

オクラ [okura] = okra, gumbo.

オムライス [omuraisu] = an omelet filled with a tomato sauce and rice mixture.

オムレツ [omuretsu] = an omelet.

オンエア [on ea] = on the air; rarely on ji ea.

23

オーライ [ōrai] = it's all right to back up; shortened from ōru raito, "all right".

オートレース [ōtorēsu] = car race, automobile race.

オートリターン [ōtoritān] = automatic arm return on a stereo.

ライム [raimu] = a lime.

ライオン [raion] = a lion.

ラム [ramu] = 1) cooked or ready-to-cook lamb. 2) rum-flavored.

シーツ [shiitsu] = bed sheet(s).

システム [shisutemu] = a popular modern-sounding word for system.

ステレオ [sutereo] = stereo set or stereophonic.

スーツ [sūtsu] = a suit, especially a woman's suit.

テラス [terasu] = a terrace.

テスト [tesuto] = one word for a school quiz or test.

ツアー [tsuā] = tour; used in compounds like sukii tsuā, a package skiing trip.

ツイン [tsuin] = 1) a hotel room with twin beds. 2) a twin bed; from tsuin beddo. 3) two-of-a-kind, as in tsuin tawā.

ツーリストクラス [tsūrisuto kurasu] = tourist class (on an airplane or ship).

ツートンカラー [tsū ton karā] = two-tone(d), having two colors.

PLACES

オンタリオ [ontario] = Ontario

オーストラリア [ōsutoraria] = Australia

オーストリア [ōsutoria] = Austria

ラオス [raosu] = Laos

ラテンアメリカ [raten amerika] = Latin America

PEOPLE

オーエン [ōen] = Owen

オーム [ōmu] = Ohm (also unit of electrical resistance)

オリリー [oririi] = O'Leary

オスカー [osukā] = Oscar

レオ [reo] = Leo (based on the spelling, so re, not ri)

24

タム [tamu] = Tam (with an ah-sound)

テーラー [tērā] = Taylor

テリー [terii] = Terry

トム [tomu] = Tom (with an oh-sound)

CHALLENGE

1. Which of the following is the correct spelling of bed sheets?
   a) シーツ b) ツーシ
2. Which of the following is the correct spelling of Taylor?
   a) ラーテー b) テーラー
3. Oakland, California and Aukland, New Zealand are spelled the same way. Which two kanas do they begin with?
4. Japanese borrowed the German word for hysteria, Hysterie. How do you think this is written in katakana?

ANSWERS

Practice:

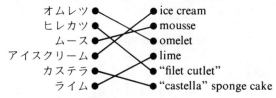

Challenge:

1. a) シーツ (shiits*u*) = sheets
2. b) テーラー (tērā) = Taylor
3. Oakland and Aukland begin with オー, (like Austria, Australia and auto).
4. Hysterie = ヒステリー (his*u*terii)

25

LESSON 6

ア	カ		タ					ラ	ワ
イ	**キ**	シ			ヒ			リ	ン
ウ	ク	ス	ツ			ム		**ル**	
エ			テ			メ		レ	
オ	コ		ト						

NEW KANAS

Study how to pronounce the following kana and practice writing them.

キ = ki, similar to the ki in kiwi.

ル = ru, similar to rue but not unlike due and Lou. The second
stroke is the same as for re, レ.

ワ = wa, similar to wah! but the lips are not rounded.

ウ = u, similar to the u's in flute and sauerkraut and the w's in
weight, kiwi and woke. The lips, however, are not rounded.
Write ', then ワ, wa.

Japanese cannot duplicate the /wu/ in wool very well: this word
becomes ūru, ウ – ル. Japanese can, however, duplicate the first two
sounds in wink, weight and woke.

Practice writing the various combinations for "wi" (u+i), "we"
(u+e), and "wo" (u+o).

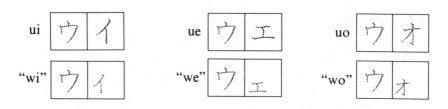

| ui | ウ イ | | ue | ウ エ | | uo | ウ オ |
| "wi" | ウ イ | | "we" | ウ エ | | "wo" | ウ オ |

RECOGNITION

The following kana are listed in Japanese alphabetical order. Write the roman spellings for each of them.

ア＿ イ＿ ウ＿ エ＿ オ＿ カ＿ キ＿ ク＿

コ＿ シ＿ ス＿ タ＿ ツ＿ テ＿ ト＿ ヒ＿

ム＿ メ＿ ラ＿ リ＿ ル＿ レ＿ ワ＿ ン＿

⟨ *a e hi i ka ki ko ku me mu n o ra re ri ru*
shi su ta te to tsu u wa ⟩

The first 5 kana in the Japanese alphabet are: a, i, u, e, o. The last 2 kana are: wa, n. Wagunā (Wagner) would be found at the end of an alphabetized group of records, under ワ (wa). Uinguzu (Wings) would be found toward the beginning, under ウ (u).

KEY WORDS

Study the following key words, then practice writing them.

wine
wa i n
ワイン

There is a native Japanese word for wine, but it won't appear on your menu or ワインリスト (wine list). Wain is also used in compounds like ワインカラー, wine-colored.

metre
mē to ru
メートル

Because メートル comes from French, (where the Metric System originated), the r-sound is retained. An alternate spelling based on British pronunciation is メーター. (メートル is a unit of measure, never a metering device.)

27

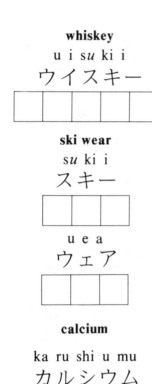

whiskey

u i s*u* ki i

ウイスキー

ski wear

s*u* ki i

スキー

u e a

ウェア

calcium

ka ru shi u mu

カルシウム

This is a very old and much-used loan-word. Some writers spell this word with a small i-kana like this; ウィスキー. There are no hard-and-fast spelling rules governing the size of the vowel kanas which combine with ウ.

The word s*u*kii refers to skis or skiing. When s*u*kii is used with the Japanese verb suru, to do, it means to ski. Wear, in the sense of clothing, is used more in Japanese than in English. Uea is often written ウエア, especially when typed on a typewriter that has no small kanas.

If you are a label-reader, katakana will help you in much of your decoding. Keep in mind that many of these words come from written English or German, not spoken English: the u in calci*u*m is pronounced /u/, not uh.

PRACTICE

These words either appear on product labels or on menus. Match them.

ウール ●   ● calcium

カルシウム ●   ● waist (size)

アルコール ●   ● steak

ウエスト ●   ● acryl*ic*

アクリル ●   ● alcohol

ウイスキー ●   ● wool

ステーキ ●   ● won-ton *ra*men

ワンタンメン ●   ● whiskey

NEW WORDS (including Key Words)

アクリル [akuriru] = acrylic.

アンコール [ankōru] = encore!; because it comes from French, the final r-sound is retained.

アラカルト [a ra karuto] = a la carte; from French, so the r in carte is retained.

アルコール [arukōru] = alcohol or alcohol content.

アウト [auto] = he's out! (in baseball).

カクテル [kak*u*teru] = a cocktail.

カラメル [karameru] = caramel.

カルシウム [karushiumu] = calcium.

カウンター [kauntā] = 1) counter area in a restaurant or bar. 2) a counting device (for copying machines, etc.).

キリン [kirin] = Kirin (brewery); all Japanese breweries' names are written in katakana.

キス [kis*u*] = a passionate kiss; kis*u* suru means to kiss passionately.

キウィ [kiui] = kiwi fruit or kiwi bird.

コルク [koruk*u*] = cork; from Dutch, so the r is retained.

メーター [mētā] = 1) a metering device. 2) another word for mētoru (100cm); based on British pronunciation.

メートル [mētoru] = a metre, 100cm; from French mètre.

オイルタンク [oiru tank*u*] = an oil tank.

オランウータン [oranūtan] = an orangutang; from Malay to Dutch to Japanese.

オールスター [ōru s*u*tā] = all-star game or all-star cast.

ルール [rūru] = an informal word for rules.

シルク [shiruk*u*] = a stylish word for silk.

スキー [s*u*kii] = skis, skiing; skii suru means to ski.

スキーウェア [s*u*kii uea] = ski wear, skiing clothes.

ステーキ [s*u*tēki] = ready-to-eat steak.

ストライキ [s*u*toraiki] = a walkout, strike; usually s*u*to.

ストライク [s*u*toraik*u*] = a strike in baseball.

タイム [taimu] = 1) thyme. 2) time clocked in sports or measured in music.

タイル [tairu] = a tile.

タオル [taoru] = towel; borrowed a long time ago from spoken, not written, English.

タレントスカウト [tarento sukauto] = a talent scout.

タウンウェア [taun uea] = city or "town" clothes.

タワー [tawā] = modern tower(s), as in tōkyō tawā, the Tokyo Tower, and tsuin tawā, twin towers.

テキ [teki] = beefsteak; shortened from French bifteck.

テキスト [tekisuto] = a modern word for textbook.

テークアウト or テイクアウト [tēkuauto] = modern word for take-out food service.

ウエスタン [uesutan] = a Western movie or song.

ウエスト [uesuto] = waist measurement; measurement of waist, hip, and bust came to Japan with Western-style clothes.

ウエートレス or ウェイトレス [uētoresu] = a waitress in a Western-style restaurant or coffeeshop.

ウインク [uinku] = a wink; uinku suru means to wink.

ウイルス [uirusu] = a virus; from German where v is pronounced w.

ウイスキー [uisukii] = whiskey.

ウクレレ [ukurere] = ukulele.

ウール [ūru] = wool removed from the sheep.

ワイン [wain] = Western-type wine, not sake.

ワインカラー [wain karā] = wine-color(ed), burgundy red.

ワインリスト [wain risuto] = a wine list.

ワンタン [wantan] = won-ton soup; from Chinese wantun.

ワンタンメン [wantanmen] = won-ton ramen soup; Chinese mien = noodles.

ワルツ [warutsu] = a waltz.

PLACES

アイオワ [aiowa] = Iowa
クウェート [kuuēto] = Kuwait

メキシコ [mekishiko] = Mexico
オタワ [otawa] = Ottawa
シアトル [shiatoru] = Seattle
トルコ [toruko] = Turkey, Turkish (also means a Turkish bath)
ウェリントン [uerinton] = Wellington
ウィーン [uiin] = Vienna (from German Wien)
ウィスコンシン [uisukonshin] = Wisconsin
ワイキキ [waikiki] = Waikiki
ワシントン [washinton] = Washington

PEOPLE

イワン [iwan] = Ivan (Russian pronunciation)
カール [kāru] = Carl
カルメン [karumen] = Carmen (from Spanish, so the r is retained)
キース [kiisu] = Keith
キーツ [kiitsu] = Keats
キム [kimu] = Kim
キリスト [kirisuto] = Christ (from Portuguese)
ルイ [rui] = Louis (French pronunciation)
ルイス [ruisu] = Lewis
ウェストン [uesuton] = Weston
ウィリアム [uiriamu] = William

CHALLENGE

1. If you have a Japanese phonebook on hand you can find this word on one of the first pages: コレクトコール. What does it mean in English?

2. Some katakana words have numerous correct spellings. What are the correct English spellings of these three words? a) キウィ, キーウィ, キィーウィ b) ウエーター, ウェイター, ウェーター c) ワルター, ウォールター

3. These words come from French and German, not English. What are these words in English? French: メートル, アラカルト, アンコール, メルシー German: ウイルス, ウィーン

4. All of these words have one kana in common: steak, text, Mexico and Christ. Which kana is it?

ANSWERS

Practice:

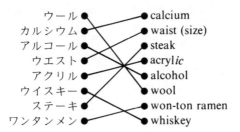

ウール ● — ● calcium
カルシウム ● — ● waist (size)
アルコール ● — ● steak
ウエスト ● — ● acryl*ic*
アクリル ● — ● alcohol
ウイスキー ● — ● wool
ステーキ ● — ● won-ton ramen
ワンタンメン ● — ● whiskey

Challenge:

1. collect call
2. a) kiwi b) waiter c) Walter
3. metre (meter), a la carte, encore, merci; virus, Vienna.
4. The k-sound in these words is spelled with キ, ki.

LESSON 7

ア	カ		タ					ラ	ワ
イ	キ	シ	**チ**	ヒ				リ	ン
ウ	ク	ス	ツ			ム		ル	
エ	**ケ**	**セ**	テ			メ		レ	
オ	コ		ト						

NEW KANAS

Study how to pronounce the following kana and practice writing them.

セ = se, similar to the se in segment.

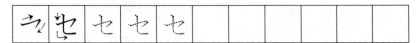

ケ = ke, similar to the ke in keg.

チ = chi, similar to the chi in chief.

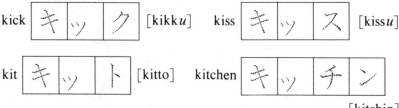

A small tsu, ッ, doubles the time it takes to pronounce the following consonant.

kick [kikk*u*]   kiss [kiss*u*]

kit [kitto]   kitchen [kitchin]

Compare the small tsu's above to the large tsu below.

Keats [kiits*u*]

33

RECOGNITION

The following kana are listed in Japanese alphabetical order. Write the roman spellings for each of them.

ア＿ イ＿ ウ＿ エ＿ オ＿ カ＿ キ＿ ク＿ ケ＿

コ＿ シ＿ ス＿ セ＿ タ＿ チ＿ ツ＿ テ＿ ト＿

< *a chi e i ka ke ki ko ku o se shi su ta te to tsu u* >

チ is never pronounced ti, but some roman spelling systems spell it ti. It comes between ta and tsu in the Japanese alphabet.

A small tsu, ッ, is not pronounced tsu, but it is alphabetized as if it were. キス (kisu) is alphabetized under ki+su, but キッス (kissu) is alphabetized under ki+tsu, between キック (kikku) and キッチン (kitchin).

KEY WORDS

Study the following key words, then practice writing them.

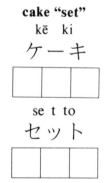

"cutlet" lunch

ka tsu   ra n chi

カ ツ　ラ ン チ

The word ランチ refers to a reasonably-priced fixed lunch special. These specials include bread or rice, coffee or tea, and sometimes soup or salad. They are available only during lunchtime hours.

cake "set"

kē ki

ケ ー キ

se t to

セ ッ ト

ケーキ refers only to Western-style cakes. セット means a fixed menu. A kēki setto is a piece of cake served with coffee or tea at a reduced price. A katsu setto is the same as a katsu ranchi, but not limited to the lunch hour.

truck *or* **track**

to ra k k*u*

トラック

Often original short-vowel sounds like those in tr*u*ck, tr*a*ck, s*e*t, k*i*ck, c*oo*kie, and h*o*t are indicated by doubled consonants in katakana. Torakk*u* meaning a lorry is a very common loan word from American English. Torakk*u* also refers to tracks used in sports.

centimetre *or* **sentimental**

se n chi

センチ

The sound /ti/ is not native to Japanese and is often replaced with チ, chi. Senchi-mētoru (centimetre) and senchimentaru (sentimental) share the same abbreviation: センチ. Senchi(mentaru) is a na adjective. (When used to describe a noun, it must be followed by the Japanese particle na.)

PRACTICE

Each of the following words have one thing in common with senchi. Match each word to its English equivalent.

チーム ●

リットル ●

アクセル ●

セクシー ●

チケット ●

スケートリンク ●

シック ●

カラット ●

SHORTENED WORDS
● accel*erator*
● skat*ing* rink

CHI FOR TI WORDS
● team
● ticket

UNITS OF MEASURE
● litre
● carat

NA ADJECTIVES
● sexy
● chic

NEW WORDS (including Key Words)

アイススケート [ais*us*u*k*ēto] = ice-skating or ice skates.

アクセント [ak*u*sento] = (foreign) accent.

アクセル [ak*u*seru] = the accelerator, gas pedal of a car.

アンケート [ankēto] = a questionnaire; from French enquête.

チーム [chiimu] = an extremely popular word for team.

チームワーク [chiimuwāk*u*] = teamwork.

チータ [chiita] = a cheetah.

チケット [chiketto] = a stylish word for a concert, theater or airline ticket.

チキン [chikin] = chicken prepared Western-style.

チキンカツ [chikin kats*u*] = a cut of chicken breaded and deep-fried.

チンキ [chinki] = tincture (medicinal solution); full form is chinki-chūru from Dutch tinctuur.

エッセイ or エッセー [essē] = a short essay.

ヒット [hitto] = 1) a hit song, movie, etc. 2) a hit in baseball.

カラット [karatto] = carat (gems) or karat (gold).

カセット [kasetto] = casette tape, film, cartridge, etc.

カツランチ [katsu ranchi] = a lunch special with *katsuretsu.*

カット [katto] = 1) a hair cut. 2) used with suru it means to cut out, delete (words).

ケーキ [kēki] = Western-style cake.

ケーキセット [kēki setto] = cake with coffee or tea special.

キック [kikk*u*] = a kick in football or soccer; with suru, to kick a ball.

キッス [kiss*u*] = a passionate kiss; alternate spelling for kis*u.*

キッチン [kitchin] or キチン [kichin] = a modern kitchen, usually with a dining area.

キット [kitto] = one word for a do-it-yourself kit.

コーチ [kōchi] = a sports coach, coaching; used with suru, to coach.

コック [kokk*u*] = a cook in a Western or Chinese restaurant; from Dutch kok.

コーンスターチ [kōns*u*tāchi] = cornstarch.

クッキー [kukkii] = a cookie.

クラッカー [kurakkā] = 1) crackers. 2) firecrackers.

クラシック [kurashikku] = Western classics, classical music.

クラッチ [kuratchi] = a (car) clutch.

メンチカツ [menchi katsu] = minced meat (usually pork) covered with breadcrumbs and deep-fried; from "minced" + "cutlet".

オーケストラ [ōkesutora] = an orchestra.

ラケット [raketto] = (tennis) racket.

ラッカー [rakkā] = lacquer.

ラック [rakku] = 1) a magazine rack. 2) shellac.

ランチ [ranchi] = daily lunch special, beverage included.

レッスン [ressun] = a modern word for lesson.

リラックス [rirakkusu] = to relax and feel at ease; always used with suru.

リットル [rittoru] or リッター [rittā] = a liter; from French litre.

ルーレット [rūretto] = roulette; with suru, to play roulette.

セイコー [seikō] = Seiko (the brand name).

セクシー [sekushii] = sexy; when followed by a noun it takes na.

セメント [semento] = cement.

センチ [senchi] = 1) a centimetre. 2) sentimental; takes na.

センチメンタル [senchimentaru] = sentimental; when followed by a noun it takes na.

センチメートル [senchimētoru] or センチメーター [senchimētā] = centimetre; usually senchi.

センター [sentā] = 1) a center, as in herusu sentā, a recreational health center. 2) center field(er) (sports).

セーラー [sērā] = sailor blouses worn by Japanese schoolgirls.

セレクター [serekutā] = selector switch.

セール [sēru] = special sale, as in kurisumasu sēru, a Christmas sale.

セーター [sētā] = a sweater, a jersey.

セット [setto] = 1) special "set" menu which includes at least a beverage. 2) a unit as in sutereo setto, stereo set. 3) set position on timers, heaters, etc; used with suru it means to set a timer, heater, one's hair, etc.

シック [shikku] = chic, stylish; takes na.

スチームカーラー [*su*chiimu kārā] = steam hair curler.
スイッチ [suitchi] = an on/off switch.
スケッチ [*su*ketchi] = a sketch; with suru, to sketch.
スケート [*su*kēto] = skating or skates; with suru, to skate.
スケートリンク [*su*kēto rink*u*] = a skating rink.
スコッチウイスキー [*su*kotchi uis*u*kii] = Scotch whiskey; often
    shortened to *su*kotchi.
スラックス [surakk*usu*] = women's slacks.
ステンレス スチール [*su*tenres*u su*chiiru] = stainless steel.
スーツケース [sūts*u*kēs*u*] = a suitcase.
トイレット [toiretto] = restroom; usually toire except in certain com-
    pounds like toiretto pēpā, toilet paper.
トラック [torakk*u* = 1) a truck, lorry. 2) sports track.
ウェットスーツ [uetto sūts*u*] = a wet suit.
ウォッカ [uokka] = vodka; from Russian where v is w.
ワックス [wakk*usu*] = wax for skis, surfboards, cars or floors.
ワクチン [wak*u*chin] = vaccine; from German where v is w.
ワセリン [waserin] = vaseline; from German where v is w.

PLACES

チリ [chiri] = Chile
カラチ [karachi] = Karachi
ケンタッキー [kentakkii] = Kentucky
セントルイス [sentoruis*u*] = St. Louis
タヒチ [tahichi] = Tahiti

PEOPLE

エセル [eseru] = Ethyl (based on English pronunciation)
ケイ [kei] = Kay
ケント [kento] = Kent
ケリー [kerii] = Kelly
ケート or ケイト [kēto] = Kate
ラッセル [rasseru] = Russell

38

リッキー [rikkii] = Ricky
リッチ [ritchi] = Rich
セレスト [seres*u*to] = Celeste

CHALLENGE

1. If you don't like singing, then avoid establishments with this word outside: カラオケ. Kara means empty in Japanese. Which 6-kana word from the list do you think oke comes from?
2. The Kunreishiki romanization system spells Tahiti like this: tahiti. The Hepburn system spells it like it is pronounced: tahichi. Change the following Kunreishiki spellings into Hepburn spellings.
   a) tiketto b) katu ranti c) sekusii
3. Somehow the word concentric got borrowed to mean an electric outlet or socket. This word was shortened to 5 kanas. How do you think it is spelled in katakana?
4. ウェット is a na-adjective that describes someone soft and tender-hearted. What English word do you suppose it came from?
5. The English name Ethyl is eseru in katakana. Ethyl alcohol, however, is echiruarukōru. Can you guess why these Ethyl's are spelled differently?

ANSWERS

Practice:

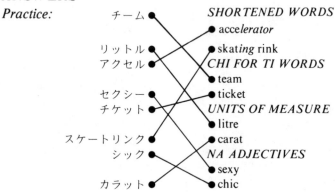

チーム●
リットル●
アクセル●
セクシー●
チケット●
スケートリンク●
シック●
カラット●

SHORTENED WORDS
●acce*lerator*
●skat*ing* rink
CHI FOR TI WORDS
●team
●ticket
UNITS OF MEASURE
●litre
●carat
NA ADJECTIVES
●sexy
●chic

39

Challenge:

1. oke comes from オーケストラ (orchestra)
2. a) chiketto (ticket) b) katsu ranchi ("cutlet" lunch) c) sekushii
   (sexy) 3. コンセント (konsento) 4. from "wet"
5. Echiruarukōru comes from German where "th" is pronounced t.
   German "Äthyl" was treated as "etil" and became echiru.

LESSON 8

ア	カ		タ	ナ				ラ	ワ
イ	キ	シ	チ		ヒ	ミ		リ	ン
ウ	ク	ス	ツ		フ	ム		ル	
エ	ケ	セ	テ			メ		レ	
オ	コ		ト						

NEW KANAS

Study how to pronounce the following kana and practice writing them.

ㄱ =fu, often *fu* (f'). Similar to the fu in kung fu, but the f is very weak, like the candle-blowing sound in whew! The u is usually silent at the ends of phrases or before t, s, k, h.

フ	フ	フ	フ						

ナ =na, similar to the na in Nazi. Try not to confuse it with メ, me.

ナ	ナ	ナ	ナ	ナ					

ミ =mi, similar to the mi in do-re-mi.

ミ	ミ	ミ	ミ	ミ	ミ				

ティ =ti, similar to the ti's in tuttifrutti. This is a special, modern spelling for a sound that is not native to Japanese. (Some older people might confuse this with テイ, tei or チ, chi.)

ティ	ティ	ティ					

RECOGNITION

The following kana are listed in Japanese alphabetical order. Write the roman spellings for each of them.

イ＿　ケ＿　セ＿　タ＿　チ＿　ツ＿　テ＿　ティ＿　ト＿　ナ＿

ヒ＿　フ＿　ミ＿　ム＿　メ＿　ラ＿　リ＿　ル＿　レ＿　ン＿

⟨ *chi fu hi i ke me mi mu n na* ⟩
⟨ *ra re ri ru se ta te ti to tsu* ⟩

フ is not pronounced hu, but some roman spelling systems spell it hu.

ティ, ti, is alphabetized under テ, te. チーム (team) comes before ティー, (tea) in Japanese dictionaries.

ナ, na and ン, n are not alphabetized next to each other.

KEY WORDS

Study the following key words, then practice writing them.

"snack"

su na k k*u*

スナック

Most Japanese think of スナック as a bar for drinking and eating light meals. Sunakk*u* can also refer to snack foods, like ナッツ (processed nuts).

terminal

tā mi na ru

ターミナル

ターミナル means a bus terminal. Tokyo's airport limousine bus terminal is called City Air Terminal in English, and シティーターミナル or シティーエアターミナル (shitii ea tāminaru) in Japanese.

MITI

mi ti

ミティ

MITI stands for the Japanese Ministry of International Trade and Industry. It can be spelled either MITI or ミティ, but it is always pronounced mi-ti. ナトー (natō) is an alternate spelling of NATO. The closest Japanese can come to /hu/, is /fu/, and that is why WHO is フー (fū) in Japanese.

"oyster" fry

"ka ki"   fu ra i

かき   フライ

| か | き | | | |

Kaki furai is an order of fried oysters. Sometimes kaki is written in katakana (カキ) instead of hiragana (かき) to attract attention. A ミックスフライ ("mixed fry") is a dish of assorted, deep-fried seafood.

PRACTICE

Two of the following words could help you get to Narita airport. The other words name organizations, foods, or drinks. Match each word to its English equivalent.

フランクフルト ●   ● City *Air* Terminal
アイスティー ●   ● Skyliner (express to Narita)
ミックスフライ ●   ● milk
ミティ ●   ● iced tea
ミルク ●   ● frankfurt*er*
ナトー ●   ● seafood "mixed fry"
シティーターミナル ●   ● MITI
フー ●   ● NATO
スカイライナー ●   ● WHO

NEW WORDS (including Key Words)

アイスミルク [aisu miruk*u*] = cold milk, sometimes with ice cubes.
アイスティー [ais*u* tii] = Western-style ice(d) tea.
アンテナ [antena] = a T.V. antenna.
アルミ [arumi] = alumin(i)um; more common than the full form, aruminiumu.
エナメル [enameru] = 1) enamel, enameled. 2) patent leather.
フー or WHO [fū] = WHO, World Health Organization.
フライ [furai] = 1) deep-fat fried, sometimes breaded. 2) a fly ball.
フランク [furank*u*] = a person or person's speech that is frank, direct; takes na.

43

フレンチトースト [furenchi tōs*u*to] = French toast.

フリー [furii] = 1) freelancing. 2) free in the sense of unhindered, as
    in furii kombāsēshon, free (unstructured) conversation.

フリースタイル [furiis*u*tairu] = freestyle (swimming, wrestling).

フルート [furūto] = Western flute.

フルーツ [furūts*u*] = fruit; used only in compounds.

フルーツケーキ [furūts*u*kēki] = fruitcake.

フットライト [futtoraito] = footlights.

ヒスタミン [his*u*tamin] = histamine.

インフレ [infure] = inflation; from infurēshon.

カフス [kaf*u*s*u*] = cuff(s).

かきフライ or カキフライ [kaki furai] = fried oysters; from "oyster"
    + "fri*ed*".

カリフラワー [karifurawā] = cauliflower.

ココナッツ [kokonatts*u*] = coconut, coconut-flavored.

コーナー [kōnā] = special areas or "corners" in stores or banks.

コーンフレーク [kōnfurēk*u*] = 1) corn flakes. 2) a general word
    for cold breakfast cereal.

ミックスフライ [mikk*u*s*u* furai] = assorted, breaded and deep-fried
    seafood; from "mix*ed*" + "fri*ed*".

ミラー [mirā] = mirror; used only in compounds like bakku mirā,
    a rearview mirror.

ミリメートル [mirimētoru] or ミリメーター [mirimētā] = millime-
    ter.

ミリリットル [miririttoru] or ミリリッター [miririttā] = milliliter.

ミルク [miruk*u*] = milk, often refers to processed (condensed,
    heated or iced) milk.

ミルクティー [miruk*u* tii] = tea with milk rather than with lemon.

ミシン [mishin] = a sewing machine.

ミス [mis*u*] = 1) Miss, as in misu amerika, Miss America. 2) a
    (spelling) mistake; with suru, to make a (minor) mistake.

ミステリー [mis*u*terii] = a mystery novel, movie, etc.

ミティ or MITI [miti] = MITI, Japanese Ministry of International
    Trade and Industry.

ナイフ [naif*u*] = a table knife used with a fork (not a kitchen knife).

ナイター [naitā] = a baseball game played at night; from twi-nighter.

ナイティー [naitii] = a nightie, found in the naito uea kōnā of a department store.

ナレーター [narētā] = a narrator.

ナトー or NATO [natō] = NATO, North Atlantic Treaty Organization.

ナッツ [natts*u*] = ready-to-eat, processed nuts.

オフレコ [ofu reko] = off the record; from ofu za rekōdo.

オートミール [ōtomiiru] = oatmeal.

ライフスタイル [raif*u*s*u*tairu] = a modern word for lifestyle.

セミクラシック [semikurashikk*u*] = semi-classical music.

セミナー [seminā] = a seminar; also zemi or zemināru from German.

シティー(エア)ターミナル [shitii (ea) tāminaru] = city terminal for airport-bound limousine buses.

スカーフ [s*u*kāf*u*] = a scarf.

スカイライナー [s*u*kairainā] = the Skyliner (express train from Ueno station to Narita airport).

スナック [sunakk*u*] = 1) a bar for drinking and eating light meals. 2) a snack.

スタッフ [s*u*taff*u*] = (company) staff members, the staff.

スタミナラーメン [s*u*tamina rāmen] = vitamin-enriched ramen soup; "stamina" + "ramen".

タフ [taf*u*] = a tough person in the sense of robust and strong; takes na.

ターミナル [tāminaru] = a bus terminal.

ティー [tii] = 1) (dark) tea; used mostly in compounds like ais*u* tii. 2) a golf tee.

トーナメント [tōnamento] = a tournament.

トレーナー [torēnā] = 1) a sweatshirt. 2) a trainer (coach).

ツナ [tsuna] = canned tuna; sometimes called shii chikin, "sea chicken" or chūna.

ウインナコーヒー [uinna kōhii] = coffee served with whipped cream; from "Vienna" + "coffee".

ワッフル [waffuru] = a waffle.

ワイフ [waif*u*] = a casual, modern word for one's own wife.

PLACES

アフリカ [afurika] = Africa

フランクフルト [franku*f*uruto] = Frankfurt (also means a frankfurter sausage)

フランス [furans*u*] = France

キエフ [kief*u*] = Kiev

オアフ [oaf*u*] = Oahu

ウェストミンスター [ues*u*tomins*u*tā] = Westminster.

PEOPLE

アンナ [anna] = Anna

エイミー [eimii] = Amy

エミリー [emirii] = Emily

フランシス [furanshis*u*] = Francis

フーリエ [fūrie] = Fourier (from French)

キティー [kitii] = Kitty

クリフ [kurif*u*] = Cliff

クリスティナ [kuris*u*tina] = Christina

ミラー [mirā] = Miller

ナンシー [nanshii] = Nancy

ナタリー [natarii] = Natalie

スミス [sumis*u*] = Smith

タミー [tamii] = Tammy

ティム [timu] = Tim

ウルフ [uruf*u*] = Woolf

CHALLENGE

1. What do you think a ミルクセーキ is?

2. If you were looking for a Frank Sinatra record, it could be listed under Frank or Sinatra. How would you spell Frank Sinatra in Japanese?

3. How would you spell Timmy?

4. All of these words begin with the same kana in Japanese: hula hoop and hurray! hurray! Which kana is it?

5. The word runner is spelled with two n's in Japanese. How do you think it is spelled?

ANSWERS

Practice:

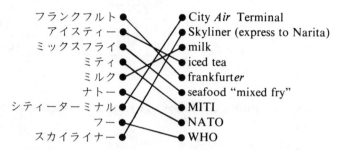

フランクフルト — City *Air* Terminal
アイスティー — Skyliner (express to Narita)
ミックスフライ — milk
ミティ — iced tea
ミルク — frankfurt*er*
ナトー — seafood "mixed fry"
シティーターミナル — MITI
フー — NATO
スカイライナー — WHO

Challenge:

1. A miruk*u* sēki is a shaken mixture of milk, egg, sugar and vanilla. It comes from "milk shake" (the sound /she/ is not native to Japanese, so /se/ was substituted).
2. Frank＝フランク (furank*u*) Sinatra＝シナトラ (shinatora)
3. Timmy＝ティミー (timii)
4. fura fūp*u* and furē! furē! begin with フ, fu
5. runner＝ランナー (rannā).

47

LESSON 9

ア	カ		タ	ナ	ハ			ラ	ワ
イ	キ	シ	チ		ヒ	ミ		リ	ン
ウ	ク	ス	ツ		フ	ム		ル	
エ	ケ	セ	テ			メ		レ	
オ	コ		ト	**ホ**			**ロ**		

NEW KANAS

Study how to pronounce the following kana and practice writing them.

ハ = ha, as in ha-ha!

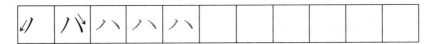

ホ = ho, similar but shorter than the ho's in hoe and horn.

ロ = ro, similar to the ro in roar but not unlike doe and low. The last two strokes are the same as コ, ko.

A recent spelling innovation enables Japanese to approximate the first two sounds in *fa*ther, *fi*at, *fe*ign and *fo*reign.

Practice writing the special combinations for fa (fu + a), fi (fu + i), fe (fu + e) and fo (fu + o). The original u-sound is not pronounced in these syllables and the f-sound is rather weak.

fa ファ　fi フィ　fe フェ　fo フォ

RECOGNITION

The following kana are listed in Japanese alphabetical order. Write the roman spellings for each of them.

ア＿ キ＿ ス＿ テ＿ ティ＿ ト＿ ナ＿ ハ＿

ヒ＿ ファ＿ フィ＿ フ＿ー フェ＿ フォ＿ ホ＿ ム＿

ラ＿ リ＿ ル＿ レ＿ ロ＿ ワ＿ ン＿

⟨ *a fa fe fi fo fū ha hi ho ki mu n*
na ra re ri ru ro su te ti to wa ⟩

フ is not pronounced hu, but it is alphabetized in the middle of the h-words. Words beginning with fa, fi, fu, fe and fo are found under フ.

KEY WORDS

Study the following key words, then practice writing them.

"roast ham"

rō s*u* ha mu

ロース ハム

Sometimes roast is ロースト, sometimes it is ロース. ロースハム is a cut of cooked ham which is more expensive than ordinary ハム. Hamu can refer to amateur radio as well as to cured ham.

home or *plat*form

hō mu

ホーム

In baseball this word means home base. This is also used in many compounds, like ホームウェア (clothes to wear at home) and ホームテレホン (telephone for home use). When you see this on a sign in a train station it means platform. (Alternate forms, purattofōmu and purattohōmu, are rarely used.)

film

fi ru mu

フィルム

Since there are so many film shops in Japan it is difficult to avoid seeing this word if you live in Japan. Unsurprisingly enough color film is カラーフィルム and roll film is ロールフィルム.

49

caffeine

ka fe i n

カフェイン

コーヒー (coffee) became an established Japanese word long before the special f-kanas were created. カフェイン (which comes from German Kaffein), and カフェオレ (from French cafe au lait) are much newer loan words.

PRACTICE

Match the following words to their English equivalents.

ホットコーヒー ●   ● hotel
ローファットミルク ●   ● coin-*operated* locker
ホテル ●   ● color film
セロハン ●   ● hi-fi
フロント ●   ● hot coffee
ハイ・ファイ ●   ● low fat milk
コインロッカー ●   ● cellophane
カラーフィルム ●   ● front *desk*

NEW WORDS (including Key Words)

アイロン [airon] = clothes iron.

アイスホッケー [aisu hokkē] = ice hockey; used with suru, to play ice hockey.

アロハ [aroha] = Hawaiian shirt; shortened from "Aloha shirt".

アルミホイル [arumi hoiru] = aluminum (tin) foil.

アスファルト [asufaruto] = asphalt.

アットホーム [atto hōmu] = cozy and comfortable, not literally at one's home; na adjective.

エロチック [erochikku] = erotic; when shortened to ero it becomes slang.

ファイル [fairu] = a file (folder) or filing cabinet; with suru, to file.

ファクシミリ [fakushimiri] = a facsimile; fakkusu for short.

ファミリーレストラン [famirii resutoran] = a family restaurant.

ファン [fan] = 1) a fan (admirer). 2) a fan built into an engine or heater (not a free-standing fan).

ファンレター [fan retā] = fan mail; from "fan" + "letter".

ファスナー [fasunā] = a fastener.

ファースト [fāsuto] = first base (baseball).

ファースト クラス [fāsuto kurasu] = first class (sea or air travel).

フェア [fea] = fair in the sense of a special sale with a theme.

フェリー [ferii] = a ferry.

フェルト [feruto] = felt (material).

フィー [fii] = a stylish word for a (golf) fee.

フィルム [firumu] = photographic film.

フィルター [firutā] = a filter (camera, cigarette, coffee, etc.).

フィット [fitto] = a (good/poor) fit in clothes; with suru, to fit.

フォーク [fōku] = 1) table fork; also hōku. 2) folk song.

フォルテ [forute] = forte (music); from Italian.

フォートラン [fōtoran] = Fortran computer language.

フォトストーリー [foto sutōrii] = a photo story.

フロア [furoa] = a floor in a department store.

フロント [furonto] = the front desk of a hotel or club; from "front desk".

フロート [furōto] = a float, as in kōra furōto, a cola float.

ハイエナ [haiena] = a hyena.

ハイ・ファイ [hai fai] = a hi-fi set or high fidelity.

ハイヒール [hai hiiru] = high heels.

ハイカー [haikā] = a hiker.

ハイミス [hai misu] = an old maid; from "high" (in years) + "miss".

ハイオク [hai oku] = high octane (gasoline), also hai okutan.

ハイセンス [hai sensu] = having good taste, "sense", in clothes.

ハイティーン [hai tiin] = late teens.

ハイツ [haitsu] = a popular component in the names of apartment buildings; from "heights".

ハイウェイ [haiuei] = a general word for highway often used in names of long-distance coaches.

ハム [hamu] = 1) cured ham. 2) ham radio.

ハムスター [hamus*u*tā] = a hamster.

ハンカチ [hankachi] = a handkerchief; two other forms are hankechi and hankachiif*u*.

ハローハロー [harō harō] = Japanese children's way of saying hello to foreigners; from British hallo.

ハッスル [hassuru] = (used with suru) to work hard and fast, to hussle.

ハウス [haus*u*] = house; used only in names of buildings and in compounds.

ヒッチハイク [hitchihaik*u*] = hitchhiking; used with suru, to hitchhike.

ホッケー [hokkē] = field hockey; with suru, to play hockey.

ホーク [hōk*u*] = older spelling of table fork, fōk*u*.

ホーム [hōmu] = 1) home base. 2) a train platform; from puratto-hōmu. 3) home for orphans or the elderly.

ホームシック [hōmushikk*u*] = homesick or homesickness, nostalgic.

ホームテレホン [hōmu terehon] or テレフォン [terefon] = a home telephone; terehon/terefon is used only in a few compounds.

ホームウェア [hōmu uea] = clothes worn at home; from "home" + "wear".

ホール [hōru] = 1) (concert) hall. 2) (golf) hole.

ホステス [hos*u*tes*u*] = a woman employed to sit with and entertain patrons of a bar or nightclub; from "hostess".

ホテル [hoteru] = a Western-style hotel.

ホットケーキ [hottokēki] = large Japanese-style hotcakes.

ホットコーヒー [hotto kōhii] = hot coffee, not ais*u* kōhii

ホワイトハウス [howaito haus*u*] = the White House.

ホワイトホースウイスキー [howaito hōsu uis*u*kii] = White Horse Whiskey.

インターホン [intāhon] = or インターフォン [intāfon] = an intercom or emergency service phone; from "inter-" + "phone".

カフェイン [kafein] = caffeine; from German Kaffein.

カフェオレ [kafe o re] = a cafe au lait.

カラーフィルム [karā firumu] = color film.

カロリー [karorii] = a calorie.

キロ [kiro] = a kilogram or kilometer.

キロメートル [kirométoru] or キロメーター [kirométa] = a kilometer.

コーヒーフィルター [kōhii firutā] = coffee filters.

コインロッカー [koin rokkā] = a coin-operated locker.

コロッケ [korokke] = a Japanese-style croquet, fritter.

クロム [kuromu] = chrome, chromium.

メロン [meron] = melon or melon-flavored.

ナイロン [nairon] = nylon.

オフィス [ofis*u*] = one of several words for an office.

レストハウス [res*u*to haus*u*] = tourist rest stop with souvenirs, film, food, etc.

ローファットミルク [rōfatto miruk*u*] = low fat milk.

ロケット [roketto] = 1) a rocket. 2) a locket.

ロック [rokk*u*] = rock music.

ロックンロール [rokku n rōru] = rock-n-roll music.

ロココ [rokoko] = rococo.

ローン [rōn] = 1) a loan. 2) a lawn.

ロールフィルム [rōru firumu] = roll film, film in a roll.

ロールスロイス [rōrusu rois*u*] = a Rolls Royce.

ロースハム [rōs*u* hamu] = an expensive cut of ham; from "roast" + "ham".

ローストチキン [rōs*u*to chikin] = roasted chicken.

ローティーン [rōtiin] = children 11 through 14 years old; from "low" + "teen".

セコハン [sekohan] = second-hand, used (car); also seko and sekando hando.

セロハン [serohan] or セロファン [serofan] = cellophane.

セロリ [serori] = celery.

ウエハース [uehās*u*] = wafers.

PLACES

ハイチ [haichi] = Haiti
ハワイ [hawai] = Hawaii
ホンコン [hon kon] = Hong Kong (sometimes written in Chinese characters)
オスロ [osuro] = Oslo
ロシア [roshia] = Russia
ロス [ros*u*] = L. A. (Los Angeles)
ストックホルム [s*u*tokkuhorumu] = Stockholm
トロント [toronto] = Toronto

PEOPLE

アルフィー [arufii] = Alfie
フェイ [fei] = Fay
フォークナー [fōkunā] = Faulkner
フロスト [furos*u*to] = Frost
ハインリッヒ [hainrihhi] = Heinrich (from German where the ch resembles h)
ハリー [harii] = Harry
ホイッスラー [hoissurā] = Whistler
ホ(ッ)チキス [ho(t)chikis*u*] = Hotchkiss (also means a stapler, named after
    the inventer, B. B. Hotchkiss)
ホワイト [howaito] = White
カルロス [karuros*u*] = Carlos (from Spanish)
ロイ [roi] = Roy
ローラ [rōra] = Laura
ローレンス [rōrens*u*] = Lawrence

CHALLENGE

1. This is the name of a very popular Japanese magazine: フォーカ
   ス. What English word do you think it comes from?
2. These two words appear on menus: a) アイスミルク b) ホット
   ミルク. What do you think they mean?
3. Most wh-words begin with ホ in Japanese. Which two of the
   following words are the exceptions? a) white b) whiskey c) WHO
   d) Whistler
4. Can you explain why coffee filter, which has two /fi/ sounds in
   English, is spelled with only one フィ in Japanese?

54

5. a) Does アイロン mean an iron golf club or clothes iron?

   b) What does アイアン mean?

ANSWERS

Practice:

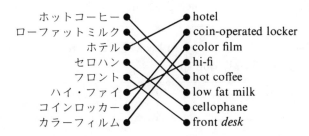

ホットコーヒー ● — ● hotel
ローファットミルク ● — ● coin-operated locker
ホテル ● — ● color film
セロハン ● — ● hi-fi
フロント ● — ● hot coffee
ハイ・ファイ ● — ● low fat milk
コインロッカー ● — ● cellophane
カラーフィルム ● — ● front *desk*

Challenge:

1. Fōkas*u* comes from the word focus.
2. a) aisu miruk*u* is cold milk, sometimes with ice cubes. b) hotto miruk*u* is warmed milk, often sweetened.
3. b) Whiskey begins with ウ. c) WHO is spelled with フ.
4. The word coffee was adopted before the fa-fi-fe-fo spelling innovation. The word filter was adopted after it.
5. a) airon＝clothes iron b) aian＝an iron golf club.

LESSON 10

ア	カ	**サ**	タ	ナ	ハ			ラ	ワ
イ	キ	シ	チ	**ニ**	ヒ	ミ		リ	ン
ウ	ク	ス	ツ		フ	ム		ル	
エ	ケ	セ	テ		**ヘ**	メ		レ	
オ	コ	**ソ**	ト		ホ			ロ	

NEW KANA

Study how to pronounce the following kana and practice writing them.

ヘ = he, similar to the he in heck. Like レ, re, and フ, fu, it is written with only one stroke.

ニ = ni, similar to the ni niece.

サ = sa, similar to the sa in saga. This is made by first writing a dash,—, then crossing it with ri, リ.

ソ = so, similar but shorter than the so's in so-so and sort. This has a final downward stroke, like ツ, tsu. Be careful not to confuse ソ, so, with ン, n.

RECOGNITION

The following kana are listed in Japanese alphabetical order. Write the roman spellings for each of them.

ア＿　カ＿　サ＿　シ＿　ス＿　セ＿　ソ＿　チ＿　ツ＿　ナ＿　ニ＿
ハ＿　ヒ＿　フ＿　ヘ＿　ホ＿　ミ＿　ル＿　レ＿　ロ＿　ン＿

⟨ *a chi fu ha he hi ho ka mi n na ni*
re ro ru sa se shi so su tsu ⟩

ニ, ni, is alphabetized with ナ, na, not with ン, n.

KEY WORDS

Study the following key words, then practice writing them.

hair tonic
he a
ヘ ア

to ni k k*u*
トニック

soft
so f*u* to
ソフト

sign
sa i n
サイン

This refers to fragranced liquid hair treatment for men (a popular item in Japan). ヘア is used in various compounds, but not on its own. トニック is used in compounds like トニックウォーター (tonic water) or on its own in the musical sense of tonic.

If your hair is supple, not hādo (hard), then look for this word on your next bottle of Japanese-made shampoo. If you are in the market for pre-recorded video tapes, then ソフト is the word to look for. Used as an adjective, sof'to takes na and can describe things like voices and personalities.

Signing one's name is an imported custom, along with autographing. サイン by itself means a signature or an autograph. Used with suru, it means to sign or to autograph. A sain bukk*u* is an autograph book.

Suntory

sa n to ri i

In many cases the English spelling of a Japanese brand name is the same as the romanization of the katakana, with the addition of a capital: キリン＝Kirin; ニコン＝Nikon; アサヒ＝Asahi. Some Japanese companies, however, are more creative with their English names: サントリー(Suntory) and ソニー(Sony) are such names.

PRACTICE

Match the following words.

テニス ●   ● concert
ヘルメット ●   ● symphony
コンサート ●   ● Sony
コンソメ ●   ● Suntory
サントリー ●   ● tennis
シンフォニー ●   ● helmet
ソニー ●   ● heli*copter*
ヘリ ●   ● consomme

NEW WORDS (including Key Words)

アクセサリー [ak*u*sesarii] ＝(fashion, automotive) accessories.

アナウンサー [anaunsā] ＝(television, radio) announcer.

アサヒ [asahi] ＝Asahi (brewery).

ハイサワー [hai sawā] ＝a drink made with *shōchū*, lemon and soda; from "hi-ball"＋"sour".

ハイソックス [hai sokk*usu*] ＝knee sock(s); from "high"＋"socks".

ハンサム [hansamu] ＝handsome (only refers to men); takes na.

ヘアスタイル [hea s*u*tairu] ＝a (Western) hairstyle; also heya s*u*tairu.

ヘアトニック [hea tonikk*u*] ＝liquid hair treatment, hair tonic; also heya tonikk*u*.

58

ヘリ [heri] =a helicopter; from herikop*ut*ā.

ヘルメット [herumetto] =a helmet.

ヘルシー [herushii] =healthy, good for you; takes na.

ヘルスメーター [herusu mētā] =a weighing machine; from "health" + "meter".

ヘルスセンター [herus*u* sentā] =a recreational health and fitness center.

カワサキ [kawasaki] =Kawasaki (the brand name).

コンサルタント [konsarutanto] =a consultant.

コンサート [konsāto] =a concert.

コンソメ [konsome] = consomme, clear soup.

コンソール [konsōru] =a (television, stereo) console.

ミキサー [mikisā] =1) a blender, liquidizer. 2) a (sound, concrete) mixer.

ミサイル [misairu] =a missile.

ニッカ [nikka] =brand of whiskey put out by Suntory, Nikka.

ニッケル [nikkeru] =nickel.

ニコチン [nikochin] =nicotine.

ニコン [nikon] =Nikon (the brand name).

ニス [nis*u*] =varnish; shortened from wanis*u*.

ニット [nitto] =knit(ted).

オニオン [onion] =onion (pronounced with o's not uh's); used only in compounds like onion sūp*u*, French onion soup.

リハーサル [rihāsaru] =a rehearsal; with suru, to rehearse.

リサイタル [risaitaru] = a recital.

サファイア [safaia] =a sapphire.

サファリ [safari] =a safari.

サーフィン [sāfin] =surfing; used with suru, to surf.

サフラン [safuran] =saffron or saffron-flavored.

サイホン [saihon] =a (coffee) syphon, siphon.

サイン [sain] =1) a signature, an autograph; used with suru, to sign one's name or autograph. 2) (sports) signals.

サイレン [sairen] =a siren, or the noise made by a siren.

サーカス [sākas*u*] =a circus.

サッカー [sakkā] = soccer; with suru, to play soccer.

サンタクロース [santa kurōsu] = Santa Claus.

サントリー [santorii] = Suntory (brewery).

サラミ [sarami] = salami.

サーロイン [sāroin] = sirloin cut of beef, cooked or uncooked.

サロン [saron] = a salon, used in names, not by itself.

サテン [saten] = satin.

サーティヴンアイスクリーム [sāti wan aisukuriimu] = 31 Flavors Ice Cream (Shop); sāti wan for short.

サウナ [sauna] = a sauna (the u is pronounced).

サワークリーム [sawā kuriimu] = sour cream.

シンフォニー [shinfonii] or シンホニー [shinhonii] = a symphony.

ソファ [sofa] = a sofa or an easy chair.

ソフト [sofuto] = 1) pre-recorded video tapes. 2) soft, supple (hair type, voice, personality, etc.); takes na.

ソフトクリーム [sofuto kuriimu] = soft whipped ice cream or ice milk.

ソフトウェア [sofutouea] = (computer) software.

ソックス [sokkusu] = a modern word for sock(s).

ソナタ [sonata] = a sonata (music).

ソニー [sonii] = Sony (the brand name).

ソロ [soro] = a solo (music).

ソテー [sotē] = saute, sauted.

テクニック [tekunikku] or テクニーク [tekuniiku] = (skiing, dating, driving) technique.

テニス [tenisu] = tennis; with suru, to play tennis.

トニック [tonikku] = (music) tonic, keynote.

トニックウォーター [tonikku uōtā] = tonic water.

ウースターソース [ūsutā sōsu] = Worcestershire sauce; sometimes usutā sōsu or just sōsu.

PLACES

アーカンソー [ākansō] = Arkansas

ヘルシンキ [herushinki] = Helsinki

60

カンサス [kansas*u*] = Kansas
カリフォルニア [kariforunia] = California
ケニア [kenia] = Kenya
サンアントニオ [san antonio] = San Antonio
サンフランシスコ [san furanshis*u*ko] = San Francisco (also shis*u*ko)
ソウル [souru] = Seoul
テヘラン [teheran] = Teheran
テキサス [tekisas*u*] = Texas

PEOPLE

アニタ [anita] = Anita
アンソニー [ansonii] = Anthony
アーサー [āsā] = Arthur
ヘンリー [henrii] = Henry
ヘレン [heren] = Helen
ヘルツ [heruts*u*] = Hertz (the unit is also spelled Hz.)
ヘッセ [hesse] = Hesse (German pronunciation)
ホイットニー [hoittonii] = Whitney
ホーソン [hōson] = Hawthorne
カサリン [kasarin] = Katherine
メラニー [meranii] = Melanie
メリッサ [merissa] = Melissa
ニコラス [nikoras*u*] = Nicholas
ニクソン [nik*u*son] or ニックソン [nikk*u*son] = Nixon
ニーナ [niina] = Nina
リサ [risa] = Lisa
サンサーンス [san sāns*u*] = Saint-Saëns
サリー [sarii] = Sally
ソフィア [sofia] = Sophia
ステファニー [s*u*tefanii] = Stephanie
ウィルヘルム [uiruherumu] = Wilhelm

CHALLENGE

1. Here are 4 different sauces. Can you identify all of them? a) ミートソース b) チリソース c) ホワイトソース d) ウースターソース
2. This is the name of a popular French pastry: クロワッサン. What is it?

3. One of the following is the correct spelling of Wilson and one is the correct spelling of consomme. Which ones are they?
   a) ウィルンソ   b) ウィルソン   c) コンソメ   d) コソンメ
4. The word for animated movies (cartoons) is only 3 kanas long and includes ニ. Can you guess what it is?
5. Tiny Chinese characters are difficult to read so some labels write their instructions in katakana. This label is a warning not to use bleach. How is エンソサラシ pronounced?

ANSWERS
Practice:

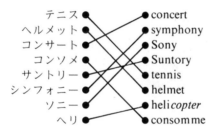

Challenge:

1. a) meat sauce b) chili sauce c) white sauce d) Worcestershire sauce.
2. クロワッサン (kurowassan)＝croissant.
3. b) ウィルソン and c) コンソメ.
4. アニメ, short for animēshon.
5. エンソサラシ＝ensosarashi (enso＝chlorine; sarashi＝bleaching)

62

LESSON 11

ア	カ	サ	タ	ナ	**パ**			ラ	ワ
イ	キ	シ	チ	ニ	**ピ**	ミ		リ	ン
ウ	ク	ス	ツ		**プ**	ム		ル	
エ	ケ	セ	テ		**ペ**	メ		レ	
オ	コ	ソ	ト		**ポ**			ロ	

P-KANAS

Study how to pronounce the following kana.

パ = pa, similar to the pa in palm.

ピ = pi, similar to the pi in piece.

プ = pu or p*u* (p'), similar to the poo in pooh. The u is usually silent when followed by t, s, k or silence.

ペ = pe, similar to the pe in peg.

ポ = po, similar but shorter than the po's in poet and port.

ン = m as in import when followed by a p, m, or b; otherwise, n as in income.

The only difference between ha, hi, fu, he, ho and pa, pi, pu, pe, po is the addition of a small circle (called maru) in the upper right-hand corner of the kana box.

Practice writing maru (°) by itself and then with the ha, hi, fu, he, ho kanas.

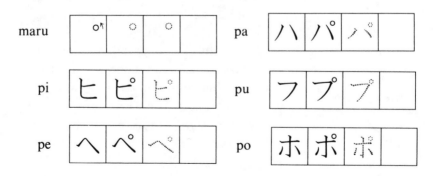

RECOGNITION

The following kana are listed in Japanese alphabetical order. Write the roman spellings for each of them.

ア＿ カ＿ サ＿ ソ＿ タ＿ ナ＿ ニ＿ ハ＿ パ＿ ヒ＿ ピ＿
フ＿ プ＿ ヘ＿ ペ＿ ホ＿ ポ＿ メ＿ ラ＿ ン＿ or n＿

⟨ *a fu ha he hi ho ka m me na ni* ⟩
⟨ *pa pe pi po pu ra sa so ta* ⟩

Words beginning with パ, pa, are alphabetized under ハ, ha; those with プ, pu, come under フ, fu, etc.

When ン is followed by any p-kana it is pronounced like the m in import. Some roman spelling systems spell this m-sound with an n.

KEY WORDS

Study the following key words, then practice writing them.

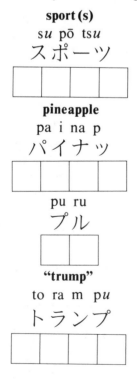

sport (s)
s*u* pō ts*u*
スポーツ

pineapple
pa i na p
パイナツ

pu ru
プル

"trump"
to ra m p*u*
トランプ

This can refer to one sport, or several sports. スポーツ now includes traditional Japanese sports (like sumo), and martial arts (like karate) as well as all Western sports.

A shorter Japanese word for pineapple is パイン. There is a native Japanese word for apple, so appuru (apple), is used only in names of Western foods prepared with apple, like アップルパイ (apple pie).

Notice how ン is pronounced m in this word. トランプ does not refer to a trump card, but apparently that is where the word came from. This word refers to Western-style cards or card-playing. One well known トランプ game is ポーカー, (poker).

"one-piece"

wa m pi i su

ワンピース

ツーピース refers to a woman's two-piece outfit. スリーピース refers to a three-piece outfit. A wampiisu is original Japanese for what we call a dress. Notice that when wan (one) is followed by p it is pronounced wam.

PRACTICE

Here are some things you are likely to find at your neighborhood スーパー (super*market*). Match them.

ヘアスプレー ●   ● popcorn
ポテトチップス ●   ● hair spray
トイレットペーパー ●   ● pineapple
アスパラ ●   ● aspara*gus*
ピーナッツ ●   ● potato chips
パイナップル ●   ● toilet paper
ポップコーン ●   ● pen
ペン ●   ● peanuts

NEW WORDS (including Key Words)

アンプ [amp*u*] = an amp(lifier).

アパート [apāto] = an apartment house which is either not modern enough nor tall enough to be called a "manshon" (page 121).

アポイント [ap_ointo] = a business appointment.

アップルパイ [appuru pai] = apple pie (usually with strudel crust).

アルプス [arup*usu*] = the (Swiss, Japan) Alps.

アスパラ [as*u*para] = asparagus; shortened from as*u*paragas*u*.

フライパン [furai pan] = a frying pan.

フラッペ [furappe] = shaved ice with syrup topping; from French frappé.

フルーツパーラー [frūts*u* pārā] = an ice cream parlor and/or fruit shop.

65

ヘアスプレー [hea supurē] = hair spray.

ヒップ [hippu] = hip measurement.

ホイップクリーム [hoippu kuriimu] = whipping cream, usually non-dairy.

インフェリオリティーコンプレックス [inferioritii kompurekkusu] = an inferiority complex, often shortened to kompurekkusu.

カップ [kappu] = 1) a measuring cup; from mejā kappu. 2) in sports it either refers to a championship cup or a golf hole cup.

カラープリント [karā purinto] = color prints from a print shop.

カセットテープ [kasetto tēpu] = a cassette tape.

コピー [kopii] = a (xerox) copy.

コピーライター [kopiiraitā] = a copywriter.

コーポ [kōpo] = a condominium; from kōporasu, "corporated" + "house".

コップ [koppu] = a glass or tumbler for cold drinks (never hot drinks); from Dutch kop.

クレープ [kurēpu] = a crepe.

ナプキン [napukin] = a napkin.

オープン [ōpun] = (grand) opening; with suru, to open a new store, building, etc.

パフェ [pafe] = a frozen parfait made with ice cream, fresh fruit and whipped cream.

パイン [pain] = common abbreviation for painappuru.

パイナップル [painappuru] = pineapple or pineapple-flavored.

パン [pan] = bread; from Portuguese.

パンク [panku] = a flat tire; from puncture.

パンティー [pantii] = women's panties.

パンツ [pantsu] = children's and men's underpants.

パパイア [papaia] = a papaya.

パーセント [pāsento] = percent, %.

パーティー [pātii] = a (Western-style) party.

パートタイム [pātotaimu] = the type of part-time job usually held by middle-aged women.

ペン [pen] = any pen except a fountain pen.

ペリカン [perikan] = a pelican.

ペット [petto] = a house pet.

ピーナッツ [piinatts*u*] = ready-to-eat peanuts.

ピンポン [pimpon] = Ping-Pong; with suru, to play Ping-Pong.

ピンク [pink*u*] = 1) pink color (preferred over native Japanese equivalents). 2) blue in the sense of "blue movie", which is pinku eiga in Japanese.

ピラフ [piraf*u*] = rice pilaff.

ポーカー [pōkā] = poker; with suru, to play poker.

ポケット [poketto] = a pocket or pocket-sized.

ポークソテー [pōk*u* sotē] = sauted pork.

ポップコーン [popp*u*kōn] = popcorn, (popped or unpopped).

ポリエステル [pories*u*teru] = polyester; from German.

ポスト [pos*u*to] = a public postbox, mailbox.

ポテトチップス [poteto chipp*u*s*u*] = potato chips, crisps; also chipp*u*.

プラスチック [puras*u*chikk*u*] = plastic, plastics.

プリン [purin] = vanilla custard; from spoken American English "pudding" (Japanese ri *is* d-like).

プリント [purinto] = a mimeographed sheet, especially a handout for students.

プロ [puro] = 1) a professional. 2) a production.

プール [pūru] = a swimming pool.

ラップ [rapp*u*] = plastic food wrap; with suru, to wrap leftovers.

サインペン [sain pen] = a felt-tipped pen; from "sign" + "pen".

サッポロ [sapporo] = Sapporo (brewery).

セロテープ [serotēp*u*] = adhesive (Scotch) tape; from the brand name Cello-tape.

シロップ [shiropp*u*] = syrup; from Dutch siroop.

スーパー [sūpā] = 1) a supermarket; from sūpāmāketto. 2) superimposed subtitles. 3) super (not regular) gasoline.

スパイ [s*u*pai] = a spy, spying, espionage; with suru, to spy.

スペル [s*u*peru] = the alphabetical spelling of a foreign word.

スピーチ [supiichi] = a formal speech.

スピーカー [supiikā] = (stereo) speaker(s).

スポーツ [supōtsu] = sport(s).

スープ [sūpu] = Western-style soup.

スプーン [supūn] = a spoon used for eating Western-style.

スリーピース [suriipiisu] = a woman's three-piece outfit.

スリッパ [surippa] = light, open-backed slippers worn inside Japanese houses, schools, etc.

スリップ [surippu] = slippery (when wet); with suru, to slip. 2) a woman's slip.

ストップウォッチ [sutoppuuotchi] = a stopwatch.

タイピスト [taipisuto] = a typist.

タイプ [taipu] = 1) a type (of person, shampoo, etc.). 2) a shortened word for typewriter; with suru, to type.

トイレットペーパー [toiretto pēpā] = toilet paper.

トップ [toppu] = leader, "top" in a race, class, etc.

トランプ [torampu] = Western cards or card-playing; with suru, to play cards; a trump card, by the way, is *kirifuda*.

ツーピース [tsūpiisu] = a woman's two-piece outfit.

ワンピース [wampiisu] = a dress; from wan, "one", + "piece".

PLACES

エチオピア [echiopia] = Ethiopia
フィリピン [firipin] = the Philippines
ミシシッピー [mishishippii] = Mississippi
パキスタン [pakisutan] = Pakistan
パリ [pari] = Paris (from French)
プエルトリコ [pueruto riko] = Puerto Rico
スペイン [supein] = Spain

PEOPLE

フィリップ [firippu] = Phillip
パトリック [patorikku] = Patrick
ピエール [piēru] = Pierre
ピーター [piitā] = Peter
ポーレット [pōretto] = Paulette
ポール [pōru] = Paul

プロコフィエフ [purokofief*u*] = Prokofiev
トンプソン [tomp*u*son] = Thompson

CHALLENGE

1. Can you guess what a ペットホテル is?
2. The word computer is often shortened to コン in compounds. Processor is sometimes shortened to プロ. What do you think these words mean in English? a) パソコン b) ポケコン c) ワープロ
3. Which word means a tumbler for cold drinks, カップ or コップ?
4. What do you think this word means? シスターコンプレックス
5. パン means different things in these words. What do you guess these words name? a) フライパン b) フランスパン c) トレパン

ANSWERS

Practice:

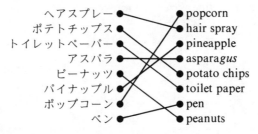

Challenge:

1. A "pet hotel" is a boarding kennel for dogs and cats.
2. a) paso kon (from pāsonaru kompyūtā) = a personal computer.
   b) poke kon (from poketto kompyūtā) = a pocket-sized computer.
   c) wā puro (from wādo purosessā) = a word processor.
3. コップ (kopp*u*) is a tumbler (kapp*u* is a measuring cup).
4. shis*u*tā kompurekk*usu* is an abnormal, but not serious, "sister complex".
5. a) furai pan = a frying pan. b) furans*u* pan = French bread.
   c) tore pan = sweat pants, gym slacks, short for "training pants".

LESSON 12

ア	カ	サ	タ	ナ	**バ**			ラ	ワ
イ	キ	シ	チ	ニ	**ビ**	ミ		リ	ン
ウ	ク	ス	ツ		**ブ**	ム		ル	
エ	ケ	セ	テ		**ベ**	メ		レ	
オ	コ	ソ	ト		**ボ**			ロ	

B-KANAS

Study how to pronounce the following kana.

バ = ba, similar to the Ba in Bach.

ビ = bi, similar to the by in baby.

ブ = bu, similar to the Bu in Buddhist.

ベ = be, similar to the be in beg.

ボ = bo, similar to the bo's in boat and bore, but shorter.

ン = m as in imbalance when followed by a b, p, or m; otherwise, n as in income.

B-kanas are made by adding two marks (called chon-chon) to ha, hi, fu, he, and ho. Practice writing chon-chon (゛) by itself and then with the ha, hi, fu, he, ho kanas.

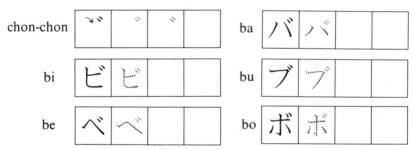

RECOGNITION

The following kana are listed in Japanese alphabetical order. Write the roman spellings for each of them.

ア__ カ__ サ__ タ__ ナ__ ハ__ バ__ パ__ ヒ__ ビ__

ピ__ フ__ ブ__ プ__ ヘ__ ベ__ ペ__ ホ__ ボ__ ポ__

ミ__ ロ__ ワ__ ン__ or n __

$$\left\langle \begin{array}{l} a\ ba\ be\ bi\ bo\ bu\ fu\ ha\ he\ hi\ ho\ ka\ mi \\ m\ na\ pa\ pe\ pi\ po\ pu\ ro\ sa\ ta\ wa \end{array} \right\rangle$$

Haydn (haidon) and Bach (bahha) are both alphabetized under ハ. Fourier (fūrie), Brahms (burāmus*u*), and Prokofiev (purokofief*u*) are all listed under フ. Beethoven (bētōben) is listed under ヘ.

When ン is followed by any b-kana it is pronounced m, never n, but some roman spelling systems spell it n.

KEY WORDS

Study the following key words, then practice writing them.

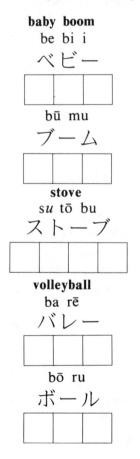

baby boom
be bi i
ベビー

bū mu
ブーム

stove
s*u* tō bu
ストーブ

volleyball
ba rē
バレー

bō ru
ボール

ベビー is not used by itself to mean a baby, but it is used in a number of compounds, such as: bebii goruf*u* (miniature golf) and bebii s*ā*kuru (a "circular" play pen). ブーム combines freely with native Japanese words to describe a sudden boom in numbers or in popularity.

オーブン refers to a cooking apparatus, an oven, but ストーブ never refers to a cooking apparatus. A ストーブ is a space heater, that is all. V-sounds are not native to Japanese and cases like sto*v*e and o*v*en, where b-kanas represent v-sounds, are very common.

Volleyball comes from America, where the sport was invented. バレー reflects American pronunciation of volley. ボール for ball, (like ホール for hall), is based on British pronunciation. Sometimes バレーボール is shortened to バレー.

service

sā bi s*u*

サービス

サービス means something extra, like a special service or a complimentary gift, that the customer does not have to pay for. A courtesy bus is a サービスバス, and copying service is コピーサービス. Guaranteed after-sales servicing is not sābis*u*, however, it is アフターサービス, "after-service".

PRACTICE

Match the words below. Four of the words below are spelled with a v in English, but a b-kana in Japanese.

ベートーベン ●   ● beer

テーブル ●   ● bacon

テレビ ●   ● volleyball

ビール ●   ● table

ベーコン ●   ● Beethoven

エレベーター ●   ● televi*sion*

バス ●   ● bus

バレーボール ●   ● elevator

NEW WORDS (including Key Words)

アフターサービス [af*u*tā sābis*u*] = after-sales service; with suru, to service or repair a product under a warranty.

アルバイト [arubaito] = the type of temporary or part-time job usually held by students; from German for work, Albeit.

アルバム [arubamu] = a photo album or record album.

バケツ [bakets*u*] = a bucket or pail (but not the kind used in Japanese bathing).

バック [bakk*u*] = 1) background scenery or experience. 2) with suru, to back up a vehicle.

バックミラー [bakku mirā] = a rearview mirror; from "back" + "mirror".

バナナ [banana] = a banana or banana-flavored.

バニラエッセンス [banira essens*u*] = vanilla extract, or "essence".

バレー or バレーボール [barē bōru] = volleyball; with suru, to play volleyball.

バレエ [baree] = ballet; accent is on the first syllable, (バレー is unaccented).

バロック [barokk*u*] = baroque music.

バス [bas*u*] = a bus or motor-coach.

バスケットボール [bas*u*kettobōru] = basketball; with suru, to play basketball.

バスタオル [bas*u* taoru] = a bath towel.

バスト [bas*u*to] = bust measurement.

バター [batā] = butter; batāk*u*sai means alien, exotic, literally "smelling of butter".

バッターボックス [battābokk*u*s*u*] = a batter's box in baseball.

ベビーブーム [bebii būmu] = the baby boom.

ベビーサークル [bebii sākuru] = a play pen; from "baby" + "circle".

ベーコン [bēkon] = cooked or uncooked bacon.

ベール [bēru] = a (wedding) veil.

ベル [beru] = a bicycle bell, school bell, station bell.

ベルト [beruto] = a belt (trousers, skirt, seat, escalator).

ビアホール [bia hōru] = a beer hall; based on British pronunciation, so beer is bia, not biiru.

ビーフ [biif*u*] = beef prepared Western-style or beef-flavored.

ビール [biiru] = beer; from Dutch bier so the r is retained.

ビニール [biniiru] = vinyl, soft vinyl plastic.

ビル [biru] = a (modern) building; can be used alone, but is usually found in the names of buildings; from birujingu.

ビスケット [bis*u*ketto] = a British-style biscuit, a cookie-like wafer.

ビタミン [bitamin] = vitamin.

ボーナス [bōnas*u*] = a semi-annual bonus paid to most Japanese employees.

ボールペン [bōru pen] = a ball-point pen.

ボタン [botan] = 1) garment button(s). 2) push buttons for elevators, street signals, etc.; from Portuguese.

ボート [bōto]＝a small rowboat, never a large boat.

ブラウス [burausu]＝a blouse.

ブレーキオイル [burēki oiru]＝brake fluid; from "brake"＋"oil".

ブルーベリー [burūberii]＝blueberries or blueberry-flavored.

ブルース [burūsu]＝blues music.

ブーツ [būtsu]＝fashionable boots (not work boots).

エレベーター [erebētā]＝an elevator, a lift.

カーブ [kābu]＝a (sharp) curve in the road (up ahead).

カフスボタン [kafusu botan]＝cuff link(s); from "cuff"＋"button".

ケース・バイ・ケース [kēsu bai kēsu]＝on a case-by-case basis.

コンバーター [kombātā]＝a converter.

コーンビーフ [kōmbiifu]＝corned beef.

コンビナート [kombināto]＝an industrial complex; from Russian kombinat.

コンビニエンスストア [kombiniensu sutoa]＝a convenience store, like Sebun Irebun (7/11).

コピーサービス [kopii sābisu]＝(Xerox) copying service.

クラブ [kurabu]＝1) an after-school or after-work "club". 2) a golf club.

ナンバーワン [nambā wan]＝the best, ♯1.

オーバー [ōbā]＝1) an overcoat; shortened from ōbākōto. 2) exaggerated, excessive; takes na. 3) with suru, to go over or exceed (the budget).

オーバーワーク [ōbāwāku]＝to work too long and too hard; with suru, to work too much.

オーブントースター [ōbuntōsutā]＝a toaster oven, a small oven.

オリーブ [oriibu]＝olives.

オートバイ [ōtobai]＝a motorcycle; shortened from ōtobaiku, "auto"＋"bike".

ピーナッツバター [piinattsu batā]＝peanut butter.

プレハブ [purehabu]＝a prefabricated house, a prefab.

ラビオリ [rabiori]＝ravioli.

ラボ [rabo]＝a language lab or film processing lab; from laboratory.

レバー [rebā]＝1) cooked or uncooked liver. 2) a lever.

リブ [ribu] =cooked or uncooked ribs.

ロビー [robii] =a hotel lobby.

ロボット [robotto] =a robot.

サービス [sābis*u*] =extra services or gifts given to customers at no extra charge.

サービスバス [sābisu bas*u*] =a courtesy bus; from "service"+"bus".

サインブック [sain bukk*u*] =an autograph book; from "sign"+ "book".

スケッチブック [s*u*ketchibukk*u*] =a sketchbook.

ストーブ [s*u*tōbu] =a space heater; from British English stove.

ストロベリー [s*u*toroberii] = strawberry-flavored or prepared with strawberries.

テーブル [tēburu] =any Western-style table.

テレビ [terebi] =a television, shortened from terebijon.

PLACES

バンコク [bankok*u*] =Bangkok

バンクーバー [bankūbā] =Vancouver

バレンシア [barenshia] =Valencia (as in Valencia oranges)

ベイルート [beirūto] =Beirut

ベルファースト [berufās*u*to] =Belfast

ベルリン [berurin] =Berlin

ベトナム [betonamu] =Vietnam

ボリビア [boribia] =Bolivia

ケベック [kebekk*u*] =Quebec

ペンシルバニア [penshirubania] =Pennsylvania

リバプール [ribapūru] =Liverpool

テルアビブ [teru abibu] =Tel Aviv

PEOPLE

バーバラ [bābara] =Barbara

バッハ [bahha] =Bach (from German)

ベバーリー [bebārii] =Beverly

ベートーベン [bētōben] =Beethoven

ベティー [betii] =Betty

ビクター [bik*u*tā] =Victor

ビル [biru] =Bill

ボイコット [boikotto] =Boycott (with suru, to boycott)

ブラームス [burāmus*u*] = Brahms
ブラウン [buraun] = Brown
ロバート [robāto] = Robert (ボブ for short)
スティーブン [s*u*tiibun] or スチーブン [s*u*chiibun] = Steven

CHALLENGE

1. The following small things are all pronounced very differently in Japanese than in English: a) ボタン, b) リボン, c) ラベル. What are they in English?
2. シルバーシート signs designate areas in trains or buses reserved for the aged or handicapped. What color are these seats?
3. What do you suppose the following "cars" and "hotels" really are? a) ケーブルカー b) ベビーカー c) ベビーホテル d) ラブホテル
4. Like in so many other loan words, the -ed in corned beef is dropped. How is this word pronounced in Japanese?
5. English numbers are sometimes used in Japanese words. How would you spell the numbers 1 through 11 in katakana?

ANSWERS

Practice:

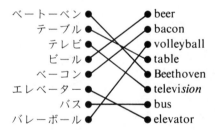

ベートーベン●	●beer
テーブル●	●bacon
テレビ●	●volleyball
ビール●	●table
ベーコン●	●Beethoven
エレベーター●	●televi*sion*
バス●	●bus
バレーボール●	●elevator

Challenge:

1. a) botan = button b) ribon = ribbon c) raberu = label.
2. shirubā = silver or silver-gray.
3. a) a cable car, a funicular. b) a baby carriage, a pram. c) a day-care center, a nursery. d) a "love hotel" or "rendez-vous" hotel (for couples without luggage).
4. kōn + biif*u* is pronounced kōmbiif*u*.
5. 1 = ワン, 2 = ツー, 3 = スリー, 4 = フォー, 5 = ファイブ, 6 = シックス, 7 = セブン, 8 = エイト, 9 = ナイン, 10 = テン, 11 = イレブン.

LESSON 13

ア	ガ	サ	タ	ナ	ハ			ラ	ワ
イ	ギ	シ	チ	ニ	ヒ	ミ		リ	ン
ウ	グ	ス	ツ		フ	ム		ル	
エ	ゲ	セ	テ		ヘ	メ		レ	
オ	ゴ	ソ	ト		ホ			ロ	

G-KANAS

Study how to pronounce the following kana. Some Japanese speakers nasalize these sounds.

ガ＝ga, similar to the ga in garment (or the nga in "long arm").

ギ＝gi, similar to the gy in Peggy (or the ngy in tangy).

グ＝gu, similar to the goo in goose and mongoose.

ゲ＝ge, similar to the ghe in spaghetti (or the nge in "Sing Eddy!").

ゴ＝go, similar to but shorter than the word go (or the ngo in hangover).

ッ＋any G-kana＝a single or double g-sound, depending on the speaker. (Doubled g's are only used in spelling foreign words, they are not used in spelling native Japanese words.)

G-kanas are made by adding chon-chon to ka, ki, ku, ke, and ko. Practice writing ga, gi, gu, ge, go.

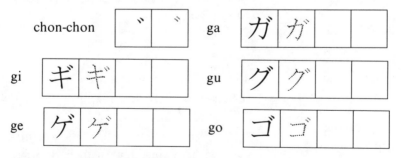

RECOGNITION

The following kana are listed in Japanese alphabetical order. Write the roman spellings for each of them.

77

ア＿　カ＿　ガ＿　キ＿　ギ＿　ク＿　グ＿　ケ＿　ゲ＿　コ＿
ゴ＿　シ＿　ツ＿　ニ＿　ヒ＿　ペ＿　ボ＿　ム＿　ル＿　ワ＿

⟨ *a bo ga ge gi go gu hi ka ke ki*
 ko ku mu ni pe ru shi tsu wa ⟩

KEY WORDS

Study the following key words, then practice writing them.

spaghetti
su pa ge t
スパゲツ

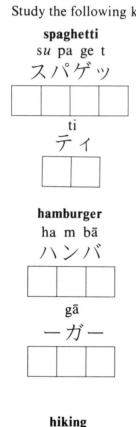

ti
ティ

Sometimes this is spelled without the small tsu: スパゲティ. A popular spaghetti dish with clams is スパゲッティボンゴレ. (Vongole is Italian for a small clam.)

hamburger
ha m bā
ハンバ

gā
ーガー

This word means a hamburger in a bun that is ready to eat. It never refers to raw ground beef. An original Japanese word related to this is ハンバーグステーキ. This is a thick cooked patty of ground meat (usually beef and pork) with sauce on top and no bun.

hiking
ha i ki n gu
ハイキング

This can be a noun, adjective, or verb (using suru). Japanese hiking trails usually have plenty of ハイキングコース signs. Words ending with ング are numerous, here are a few in their original English forms: bowling, boxing, cycling, jogging, wrestling, skin-diving and dry cleaning.

"Inglez"

i gi ri s*u*

イギリス

Some Japanese people pronounce this more like i*ng*iris*u* than i*giris u*. It originated from the Portuguese word for Englishman, Inglez. In Japanese イギリス refers to Great Britain. (The country east of Wales and south of Scotland, namely England, is ingurando in Japanese.)

PRACTICE

Match the following activities, pastimes and hobbies.

ゴルフ ●	● bowling
サイクリング ●	● guitar
ハイキング ●	● hiking
ランニング ●	● golf
ゲーム ●	● running
ボクシング ●	● boxing
ボウリング ●	● cycling
ギター ●	● game

NEW WORDS (including Key Words)

アレルギー [arerugii] = an allergy; from German Allergie which has a hard-g sound.

バーゲンセール [bāgen sēru] = a sale full of bargains.

バッグ [ba(g)gu] or バック [bakk*u*] = a handbag; some double-g words (which are all difficult to pronounce) have alternate spellings with double-k (which are easy to pronounce).

バイキング [baikingu] = 1) Viking. 2) a smorgasbord; named after the first smorgasbord restaurant in Tokyo, the Viking.

ベビーゴルフ [bebii goruf*u*] = miniature golf; from "baby" + "golf".

ボクシング [bok*u*shingu] = boxing; with suru, to box.

ボクシンググラブ [bok*u*shingu gurabu] = boxing gloves.

ボンゴレ [bongore] = small Italian-type clams.

ボーリング [bōringu] = 1) boring (for gas, oil, etc.). 2) alternate spelling for bowling.

ボウリング [bouringu] = bowling; with suru, to bowl.

エレキギター [erekigitā] = an original word for an electric guitar.

フロントガラス [furonto garasu] = car windshield, windscreen; from "front" + "pane glass".

ガム [gamu] = chewing gum; also chūingamu.

ガラス [garasu] = pane glass; from Dutch glas.

ガソリン [gasorin] = gasoline, petrol.

ガス [gasu] = natural gas.

ゲイボーイ [gei bōi] = a young homosexual man; from "gay" + "boy".

ゲーム [gēmu] = any parlor game; with suru, to play a game.

ゲリラ [gerira] = guerilla warfare.

ゲスト [gesuto] = a guest on a radio or T. V. show.

ギフト [gifuto] = one of several words for a gift or present.

ギプス [gipusu] or ギブス [gibusu] = a plaster cast; from German Gips.

ギター [gitā] = a guitar.

ゴム [gomu] = rubber, elastic, or gum from the gum tree; from Dutch gom.

ゴリラ [gorira] = a gorilla.

ゴルフ [gorufu] = golf; with suru, to play golf.

ゴールイン [gōruin] = reaching one's goal or objective; from "goal" + "in".

グラフ [gurafu] = a graph or diagram.

グラム [guramu] = a gram, 1/1000th of a kiroguramu (kilogram).

グラスワイン [gurasu wain] = wine served by the glass; from "glass" + "wine".

グラタン [guratan] = macaroni in a cream sauce cooked "au gratin".

グレービー [gurēbii] = gravy; sometimes gurēbii sōsu (sauce).

グレープ [gurēpu] = grape-flavored or prepared with grapes.

グレープフルーツ [gurēpufurūtsu] = a grapefruit.

グリーン [guriin] = 1) a putting green. 2) one of several words for green.

グリーンカー [guriin kā] = a first-class car in a train, a "green car".

グリーンピース [guriin piisu] = "green" pea(s).

グロッギー [guro(g)gii] or グロッキー [gurokkii] = groggy.

グロッシー [gurosshii] = (prints) glossy, not matt, finish.

グロテスク [gurotesuku] = grotesque; takes na.

グールメ [gūrume] = a gourmet; from French pronunciation.

グループ [gurūpu] = one word for a small group of 3-10 members.

ハイキングコース [haikingu kōsu] = hiking trail, hiking course.

ハンバーガー [hambāgā] = a ready-to-eat hamburger in a bun.

ハンバーグステーキ [hambāgu sutēki] = ground meat patty with sauce; from English pronunciation of "Hamburg" + "steak".

ハムエッグ [hamu e(g)gu] = ham and eggs.

ヘアゴム [hea gomu] = an elastic hair band.

イアリング [iaringu] = earring(s); also iyaringu.

イブニング [ibuningu] = an evening dress.

カンガルー [kangarū] = a kangaroo.

カンニングペーパー [kanningu pēpā] = a euphemism for notes used for cheating on a test; from "cunning" + "paper".

カタログ [katarogu] = a catalogue.

クリーニング [kuriinigu] = professional cleaners or cleaning; with suru, to clean professionally.

ミックスグリル [mikkusu guriru] = a platter of assorted grilled meats.

オルゴール [orugōru] = a music box; from Dutch orgel.

プラグ [puragu] = a plug.

プロゴルファー [puro gorufā] = a professional golfer.

ライスグラタン [raisu guratan] = rice in a cream sauce prepared "au gratin".

ライトグレー or ライトグレイ [raito gurē] = light gray.

ランニング [ranningu] = 1) the athletic event of running. 2) a man's sleeveless undershirt; shortened from ranningu shatsu.

レゲエ [regee] = reggae music.

レスリング [resuringu] = Western-style wrestling; with suru, to wrestle Western-style.

ロッククライミング [rokkukuraimingu] = rock-climbing.

サイクリング [saikuringu] = recreational bicycling, cycling.

サイクリングコース [saikuringu kōs*u*] = a recreational cycling course.

サングラス [sanguras*u*] = a pair of sunglasses.

シンガーソングライター [shingā songuraitā] = a singer-songwriter.

シングル [shinguru] = 1) a single scoop of ice cream, shot of whiskey, bed or single-breasted. 2) unmarried person.

シングルス [shingurus*u*] = (tennis) singles.

スパゲッティ or スパゲティ [s*u*page(t)ti] = spaghetti.

ストッキング [s*u*tokkingu] = women's stockings.

ウォーミングアップ [uōmingu app*u*] = a warm-up; with suru, to warm up before working out.

ワゴン [wagon] = the dessert "wagon" in a French restaurant.

ワイングラス [waingras*u*] = a wineglass.

PLACES

ベルギー [berugii] = Belgium (from its true name, België)
ギリシア [girishia] = Greece (from Portuguese Gresia)
グアム [guamu] = Guam
グラスゴー [gurasugō] = Glasgow
ハーグ [hāgu] = The Hague
ハンガリー [hangarii] = Hungary
イギリス [igiris*u*] = Great Britain (from Portuguese Inglez)
コペンハーゲン [kopenhāgen] = Copenhagen
オレゴン [oregon] = Oregon
ポルトガル [porutogaru] = Portugal
シカゴ [shikago] = Chicago
シンガポール [shingapōru] = Singapore

PEOPLE

アガサ [agasa] = Agatha
バン ゴッホ [ban gohho] = Van Gogh (also just gohho)
エンゲル [engeru] = Engel
グッゲンハイム [gu(g)genhaimu] = Guggenheim

グレー or グレイ [gurē] = Gray, Grey
グレゴリー [guregorii] = Gregory
グレース [gurēsu] = Grace
クレグ [kuregu] = Craig
ペギー or ペッギー [pe(g)gii] = Peggy
レーガン [rēgan] = Reagan
ワグナー [wagunā] = Wagner

CHALLENGE

1. If you want wine by the glass do you ask for a) ワイングラス or b)グラスワイン ?
2. These words have similar katakana spellings. Can you identify them?
   a) ハイキング/バイキング   b) クレープ/グレープ
   c) クラブ/グラフ
3. Write the first g-kana for each of the following words. Example: gum to chew = ガ; gum from the tree = ゴ. a) glass for window panes = __ b) a glass for wine = __ c) gorilla = __ d) guerrilla = __.
4. How is the small tsu pronounced in the following words?
   バッグ、エッグ、グロッギー、グッゲンハイム
5. Recreate some of the many ゴム words by filling in the following Japanese words: ki (tree), keshi (erase), wa (ring-shaped), in (stamp).
   a) a rubber eraser = ____ gomu b) a rubber stamp = gomu ____
   c) a rubber band = ____ gomu   d) a gum tree = gomu no ____

ANSWERS

Practice:

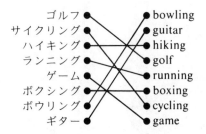

ゴルフ	bowling
サイクリング	guitar
ハイキング	hiking
ランニング	golf
ゲーム	running
ボクシング	boxing
ボウリング	cycling
ギター	game

Challenge:

1. b) gurasu wain = a glass *of* wine
2. a) hiking/Viking (smorgasbord) b) crepe/grape c) club/graph
3. a) ガ (garas*u*) b) グ (guras*u*) c) ゴ (gorira) d) ゲ (gerira)
4. Some speakers ignore the small tsu, others pronounce it as the first part of a double-g.
5. a) keshigomu (a rubber eraser) b) gomuin (a rubber stamp) c) wagomu (a rubber band) d) gomu no ki (a gum or rubber tree)

LESSON 14

ア	カ	サ	**ダ**	ナ	ハ			ラ	ワ
イ	キ	シ	チ	ニ	ヒ	ミ		リ	ン
ウ	ク	ス	ツ		フ	ム		ル	
エ	ケ	セ	**デ**		ヘ	メ		レ	
オ	コ	ソ	**ド**		ホ			ロ	

D-KANAS

Study how to pronounce the following kana.

ダ = da, similar to the da in dart.

デ = de, similar to the de in dead.

ディ = di, similar to the dy in sandy.

ド = do, similar but shorter than the do's in do-re-mi and adore.

ツ + any D-kana = a single or double d-sound, depending on the speaker.

D-kanas are made by adding chon-chon to ta, te, ti (te+i) and to. Practice writing da, de, di and do.

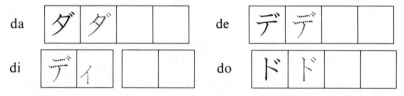

Very few borrowed words are spelled with チ (chi+ ゛). This kana is pronounced ji and appears in the name Bridgestone, ブリヂストン, and sometimes in the word building, ビルヂング.

There are no borrowed words spelled with ヅ (tsu+ ゛). A few native Japanese words might turn up with this kana when typed on a katakana typewriter, in which case ヅ would be pronounced zu (or dzu by some people).

RECOGNITION

The following kana are listed in Japanese alphabetical order. Write the roman spellings for each of them.

ウ＿　ギ＿　コ＿　ソ＿　タ＿　ダ＿　チ＿　ツ＿　テ＿　デ＿

ティ＿　ディ＿　ト＿　ド＿　ナ＿　バ＿　プ＿　ヘ＿　ミ＿

ラ＿　レ＿　ワ＿

⟨ ba chi da de di do gi he ko mi na
  pu ra re so ta te ti to tsu u wa ⟩

KEY WORDS

Study the following key words, then practice writing them.

"bed town"
be (d) do
ベッド

ta u n
タウン

This is Japanese-English for a suburban bedroom community. A ベッド refers to any Western-style bed. Most Japanese speakers pronounce ベッド as be-do, dropping the first d-sound. An alternate spelling that is easy to pronounce, but less popular, is ベット, betto.

audio
ō di o
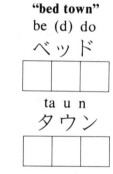
オーディオ

Wherever you see the word audio you are likely to also see the word video, ビデオ. Video is not spelled with ディ, like audio, because video is patterned after its Latin spelling, not its English pronunciation.

Holland
o ra n da

オランダ

This word, like イギリス and ギリシア, comes from Portuguese. The word for Germany, ドイツ, however, comes from the Dutch word Duits. Most words that end with a d in English end with ド, not ダ in Japanese; オランダ and サラダ (salad) are exceptions.

sandwich

sa n do

サンド

i t chi

イッチ

Equally as popular is the shorter word, サンド. Japanese sandwiches are not always what you might expect: an エッグサンド contains not egg salad, but either an omelet or hard-boiled egg; a チキンサンド might contain a chicken thigh, bone and all. You can probably guess what a カツサンド is.

PRACTICE

The following words either name things to eat with your fingers, or things to do or play (using suru). Match them.

ホットドッグ ●   ● fried chicken

ボディービル ●   ● hot dog

ポテトサラダサンド ●   ● potato salad sandwich

デート ●   ● donut

ビデオゲーム ●   ● skin diving

ドーナツ ●   ● date

スキンダイビング ●   ● video game

フライドチキン ●   ● body buil*ding*

NEW WORDS *(including Key Words)*

アメリカンドッグ [amerikan do(g)gu] = a corn dog on a stick (sometimes made of fish, not meat).

バドミントン [badominton] or バトミントン [batominton] = badminton; with suru, to play badminton.

ベッド [be(d)do] or ベット [betto] = a Western-style bed.

ベッドタウン [be(d)do taun] = a bedroom community; from "bed" + "town".

ベークドポテト [bēkudo poteto] = a baked potato.

ベランダ [beranda] = a veranda.

ビアガーデン [bia gāden] = a beer garden; also biya gāden, but never bii*ru* gāden.

ビデオディスク [bideo dis*uku*] = a video disk.

ビデオゲーム [bideo gēmu] = a video game; with suru, to play one.

ビデオレコーダー [bideo rekōdā] = video tape recorder; sometimes just bideo.

ビルディング [birudingu] or ビルヂング [birujingu] = building; also biru.

ボディービル [bodii biru] = body building; with suru, to body build.

ブランデー [burandē] = brandy.

ブレンドコーヒー [burendo kōhii] = drip coffee that is stronger than amerikan kōhii.

チキンサンド [chikin sando] = a sandwich with some form of chicken in it.

ダブル [daburu] = double scoop of ice cream, shot of whiskey, bed or double-breasted.

ダブルス [daburus*u*] = tennis doubles.

ダイニングキッチン [dainingu kitchin] = a kitchen large enough to eat in; from "dining" + "kitchen".

ダンプカー [damp*u*kā] = a dump truck; "dump" + "car"; also damp*u*.

ダム [damu] = a man-made dam.

ダンサー [dansā] = a professional dancer.

ダンス [dans*u*] = Western-style dance, dancing; with suru, to dance Western-style.

ダース [dās*u*] = a dozen (not used as much as in English).

デパート [depāto] = a department store.

デラックス [derakk*usu*] = deluxe (car, hotel); takes na.

データ [dēta] = data.

デート [dēto] = dating, a date; with suru, to date.

ディレクター [direk*u*tā] = a film director, also used in job titles.

ディスカウントセール [dis*u*kaunto sēru] = a discount sale.

ディスコ [dis*u*ko] = disco; also dis*u*kotēk*u*.

ドア [doa] = a Western-style door.

ドーナツ [dōnatsu] = a donut.

ドライ [dorai] = unsentimental, "dry" (opposite of uetto); takes na.

ドライアイス [dorai aisu] = dry ice.

ドライブ [doraibu] = a drive, driving; with suru, to take a drive.

ドライクリーニング [dorai kurīningu] = dry cleaning; with suru, to dry clean.

ドレス [doresu] = a formal dress, a gown.

ドリア [doria] = Italian-style rice pilaf.

ドル [doru] = a dollar, $.

エディター [editā] = one of various words for an editor.

エッグサンド [e(g)gu sando] = an omelet or hard-boiled egg sandwich; from "egg" + "sandwich".

フライドチキン [furaido chikin] = fried chicken.

フロアスタンド [furoa sutando] = a standing lamp, floor lamp; from "floor" + "stand".

ガイドブック [gaidobukku] = a guidebook.

ガソリンスタンド [gasorin sutando] = a gasoline (petrol) station; from "gasoline" + "stand".

ゴールデンアワー [gōruden awā] = prime time television; from "golden" + "hour".

ハンドバッグ [handoba(g)gu] = a handbag or shoulderbag used by women; also bag(g)gu and bakku.

ハンドル [handoru] = (bicycle) handle or steering wheel.

ヘッドホン [he(d)dohon] = headphones.

ホットドッグ [hotto do(g)gu] = a ready-to-eat hot dog.

カーディガン [kādigan] = a cardigan.

カード [kādo] = a greeting card or index card.

カレンダー [karendā] = a calendar.

カツサンド [katsu sando] = a sandwich containing a *katsuretsu*.

コンデンスミルク [kondensu miruku] = condensed milk.

コストダウン [kosuto daun] = a drop in production costs; from "cost" + "down".

クリームソーダ [kuriimu sōda] = an ice cream soda, not a soft drink.

メディア [media] ＝(mass) media.

メロディー [merodii] ＝a melody.

メロンソーダ [meron sōda] ＝melon-flavored soda water; often abbreviated to soda on menus.

ムード [mūdo] ＝atmosphere, mood.

オーディオ [ōdio] ＝audio.

ペンフレンド [pen furendo] ＝a pen pal; "pen"＋"friend".

ペーパードライバー [pēpā doraibā] ＝a person with a driver's license, but no car; from "paper"＋"driver".

ペットフード [petto fūdo] ＝pet food.

ポンド [pondo] ＝a pound, £ or lb.

ポテトサラダ [poteto sarada] ＝a potato salad made with mashed potatoes; not an uncommon sandwich filling.

プレーガイド [purē gaido] ＝theater or concert ticket agency; from "play"＋"guide".

レーダー [rēdā] ＝radar.

レコード [rekōdo] ＝a musical record or sports record.

サンデー [sandē] ＝an ice cream sundae.

サンドイッチ [sandoitchi] ＝two pieces of bread with anything from fried noodles to mashed potatoes in it; often sando.

サラダ [sarada] ＝a salad.

サラダドレッシング [sarada doresshingu] ＝salad dressing.

シーフードサラダ [shiifūdo sarada] ＝seafood salad.

スキンダイビング [sukindaibingu] ＝skin diving; with suru, to skin-dive.

スピード [supiido] ＝speed, speeding or speedy.

スタンドバー [sutando bā] ＝a bar where one must stand because there are no seats; from "stand"＋"bar".

ウェディングドレス [uedingu doresu] ＝a Western-style wedding gown.

ウェディングケーキ [uedingu kēki] ＝a wedding cake.

ワイド [waido] ＝expansive, spacious, large, "wide".

PLACES

アイルランド [airurando] = Ireland
ダブリン [daburin] = Dublin
ドイツ [doits*u*] = Germany (from Dutch Duits)
フィンランド [finrando] = Finland
フロリダ [furorida] = Florida
インド [indo] = India
イングランド [ingurando] = England (country south of Scotland)
カナダ [kanada] = Canada
オークランド [ōkurando] = Aukland or Oakland
オランダ [oranda] = Holland
ポーランド [pōrando] = Poland
ロンドン [rondon] = London
シドニー [shidonii] = Sydney
スコットランド [*su*kottorando] = Scotland
スウェーデン [suuēden] = Sweden

PEOPLE

アンディー [andii] = Andy
ダニエル [danieru] = Daniel
デービッド [dēbi(d)do] = David
デニー [denii] = Denny
ドーン [dōn] = Dawn
ドナルド [donarudo] = Donald
エドワード [edowādo] = Edward
ハイドン [haidon] = Haydn
オードリー [ōdorii] = Audrey
リディア [ridia] = Lydia
リンダ [rinda] = Linda
ウィンディー [uindii] = Windy

CHALLENGE

1. Both of these words come from French: a) オードブル b) オーデ コロン One is like a snack, the other is like perfume. What are they in English?
2. These are common Japanese-English expressions, what are they in English?　a) グッドアイディア b) グッドタイミング c) レ ディーファースト d) ハッピーエンド

3. The Japanese word from cider refers to an apple-flavored soft drink. The Japanese word from French cidre refers to alcoholic cider. Which of these words refers to a soft drink? a) シードル b) サイダー

4. The -ru from suru, する, combines with a katakana word to create this verb: ダブる. How is this word pronounced and what do you think it means?

5. Mei, 明, "bright" + chi, 治, "government" + ya, 屋, "shop" = 明治屋. This is the name of a famous Japanese food manufacturer and supermarket chain. This is not pronounced meichiya. It is not pronounced meidiya either, even though the English name is spelled Meidiya. How do you think it is pronounced?

ANSWERS

Practice:

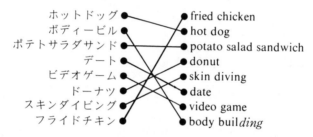

Challenge:

1. a) ōdoburu = hors d'oeuvre   b) ō de koron = eau de cologne
2. a) good idea   b) good timing   c) ladies first   c) happy end*ing*
3. b) saidā = soft-drink "cider"(shiidoru is alcoholic "cidre").
4. ダブる (dabu*ru*) = to be doubled or repeated (primarily in reference to double-faults and double plays).
5. 明治屋 is pronounced meijiya. In the middle of native Japanese words 治 (チ), chi, can change to ji, (ヂ). Since チ is sometimes spelled ti, ヂ can theoretically be spelled di, as it is in Meidiya.

LESSON 15

ア	カ	**ザ**	タ	ナ	ハ			ラ	ワ
イ	キ	**ジ**	チ	ニ	ヒ	ミ		リ	ン
ウ	ク	**ズ**	ツ		フ	ム		ル	
エ	ケ	**ゼ**	テ		ヘ	メ		レ	
オ	コ	**ゾ**	ト		ホ			ロ	

Z-KANAS

Study how to pronounce the following kana.

ザ = za, similar to the za in bazaar.

ズ = zu, similar to the word zoo, but shorter.

ゼ = ze, similar to the ze in zest.

ゾ = zo, similar but shorter than the zo's in zone and Zorba.

Z-kanas are made by adding chon-chon to sa, su, se, and so. Practice writing za, zu, ze, zo.

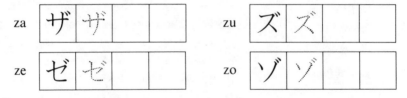

All of these pairs are related phonetically: p/b, k/g, t/d, s/z. Here are some more phonetic pairs: ch/j and sh/zh. Japanese has the ch/j pair, but lacks the zh of the sh/zh pair (zh is the middle sound in vision). Since ji is close to zhi, shi is paired with ji. The shi spelling of ji, ジ, is unquestionably more common than the chi spelling of ji, ヂ. Practice writing the preferred spelling of ji.

RECOGNITION

The following kana are listed in Japanese alphabetical order. Write the roman spellings for each of them.

エ＿　ゲ＿　サ＿　ザ＿　シ＿　ジ＿　ス＿　ズ＿　セ＿　ゼ＿
ソ＿　ゾ＿　ダ＿　チ＿　ディ＿　ト＿　ニ ゙　ピ＿　フ＿
ボ＿　メ＿　リ＿

⟨ *bo chi da di e fu ge ji me ni pi ri*
sa se shi so su to za ze zo zu ⟩

Although ジ is never pronounced zi, it is sometimes spelled zi. It is spelled dzi in the word Godzilla, and di in the name Meidiya.

KEY WORDS

Study the following key words, then practice writing them.

(imitation) leather

re zā

レ ザ ー

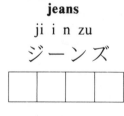

レザー can refer to genuine or imitation leather. Another word to be suspicious of is サイズ: フリーサイズ, "free size", only means one-size-fits-all if you normally wear small or medium sizes; L-サイズ, (pronounced eru saizu) is medium, not large, by Western standards.

jeans

ji i n zu

ジ ー ン ズ

A much more original Japanese word that also means jeans is jiipan, from jeans+pants (trousers). The older spelling of this word is ジーパン and the newer spelling (probably patterned after T-shirt) is G-パン. By the way, the Japanese word for trousers, ズボン, comes from the French word for petticoat, jupon (zhupon).

94

jelly
ze ri i

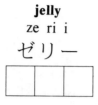

The sound /je/ is not native to Japanese. In the word jelly, /je/ has been replaced with ゼ, ze. Other words pronounced with a ze-sound in Japanese, but not in English, include: gelatine, ゼラチン, and Argentina, アルゼンチン.

transister radio
to ra n ji *su*

トランジス

tā ra ji o

タ ー ラ ジ オ

The closest Japanese sound to the /zi/ in tran*si*ster is ji. The closest *native* Japanese sound to the /di/ in ra*di*o is also ji. (Just like chi is the closest *native* Japanese sound to the /ti/ in cen*ti*meter.) ラジオ was already a common Japanese word by the 1930's, before ティ and ディ were well-enough established to be used in words like オーディオ (audio) and パーティー (party).

PRACTICE
Fill in ザ, ジ, ズ, ゼ, or ゾ in the following words.

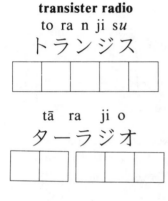

school zone   ス ク ー ル 　 ー ン

cheesecake   チ ー 　 ケ ー キ

rose wine   ロ 　 ワ イ ン

sausage   ソ ー セ ー

jeans   　 ー ン 　 lasagna   ラ 　 ニ ア

dessert   デ 　 ー ト   studio   ス タ 　 オ

NEW WORDS (including Key Words)

バドワイザー [badowaizā]＝Budweiser (brewery).

バザー [bazā]＝a (charity) bazaar.

ブレザーコート [burezā kōto]＝a blazer; the addition of kōto (coat) is not redundant in Japanese like it is in English.

ブザー [buzā]＝a buzzer.

チーズ [chiizu]＝cheese.

チーズケーキ [chiizukēki]＝cheesecake.

チンパンジー [chimpanjii]＝chimpanzee.

デジタル [dejitaru] or ディジタル [dijitaru]＝digital; デ for di preceded ディ.

デザイン [dezain]＝a modern word for design, designing; with suru, to design.

デザート [dezāto]＝a dessert.

エキゾチック [ekizochikku]＝exotic; also ekizo; takes na.

M-サイズ [emu saizu]＝small-sized clothes (by Western standards).

エンゲージリング [engējiringu]＝an engage*ment* ring.

エンジン [enjin]＝an engine.

LL-サイズ [eru eru saizu]＝extra wide, not extra long, clothes.

L-サイズ [eru saizu]＝medium-sized clothes (by Western standards).

S-サイズ [esu saizu]＝petite-sized clothes (by Western standards).

ファザコン [faza kon] ＝ an Electra (Oedipus) complex; from fāzā "father"＋kompurekku*su* "complex".

フジフィルム [fuji firumu]＝Fuji film (brand name).

フリーサイズ [furii saizu]＝one-size-fits-all (if you are small or medium); from "free"＋"size".

フリーザー [furiizā]＝a freezer or freezer compartment.

ガレージ [garēji]＝one word for a car-parking garage; patterned after British pronunciation of garage.

ガーゼ [gāze]＝gauze; from German Gaze.

グラジオラス [gurajiorasu]＝gladiolus (flowers).

イージーリスニング [iijiirisuningu]＝easy-listening music.

イメージアップ [imēji appu]＝improvement in personal or corporate appearance or "image"; can be used with suru; from "image"＋"up".

インフルエンザ [infuruenza] = the flu, influenza.

ジーンズ [jiinzu] = jeans.

ジーパン or G-パン [jiipan] = jeans; from "jeans"+"pants".

ジンフィズ [jin fizu] = a gin fizz.

ジッパー [jippā] = a zipper.

ジルバ [jiruba] = the jitterbug; like purin/pudding, the American d-sound (-tt-) is replaced with r and the final g is lost.

カテッジチーズ [kate(j)ji chiizu] = cottage cheese; pronounced with either a single or double j-sound.

カートリッジ [kātori (j)ji] = a cartridge.

コーヒーゼリー [kōhii zerii] = coffee-flavored jelly desert.

コンタクトレンズ [kontakuto renzu] = contact lenses.

クイズ [kuizu] = a radio, T. V. or magazine quiz.

クレジットカード [kurejitto kādo] = a credit card.

メッセージ [messēji] = one of several words for a message.

メゾン [mezon] = a popular element in names of apartment buildings; from French "maison", house.

オレンジ [orenji] = 1) Western-type oranges (not Japanese mikans). 2) the color orange.

オリジナル [orijinaru] = original (design, flavor, etc.); takes na.

オゾン [ozon] = ozone.

パージ [pāji] = the removal of persons associated with the old order during the American Occupation; from "purge".

ページ [pēji] = a book page.

ピザ [piza] = pizza.

プレゼント [purezento] = a popular, informal word for a present.

プロポーズ [puropōzu] = a proposal of marriage; with suru, to propose marriage.

ラジエーター [rajiētā] = a radiator.

ラジカセ [rajikase] = a combination radio-cassette recorder; from rajio+kassetto.

ラジオ [rajio] = a radio.

ラザニア [razania] = lasagna; also razanya.

レジ [reji] = 1) a cash register; from rejisutā. 2) the cashier area or the cashier.

レンジ [renji] = 1) a "range" with burners and sometimes a small fish grill, but rarely an oven. 2) a microwave oven is a denshirenji; from "electronic"+"range".

レーザー [rēzā] = laser.

レザー [rezā] = 1) genuine or imitation leather; perhaps from leatherette. 2) a razor.

リムジン [rimujin] = a limousine bus (a limousine car is usually rimujin kā).

ロッジ [ro(j)ji] = a (ski) lodge; pronounced with a single or double j-sound.

ロゼワイン [roze wain] = rose wine.

ルーズ [rūzu] = "loose" about keeping appointments, about money, about lovers; takes na.

ルーズフィット [rūzu fitto] = loose-fitting.

ルーズリーフ [rūzu riifu] = a loose-leaf binder.

サイズ [saizu] = a very common word for size of manufactured articles.

サウザンド (アイランド) ドレッシング [sauzando (airando) doresshingu] = Thousand Island salad dressing.

スクールゾーン [sukūru zōn] = school zone (used on signs).

スーパーバイザー [sūpābaizā] = one word for a supervisor.

スポンジ [suponji] = a sponge.

スタジオ [sutajio] = a studio for recording, filming, etc.

トランジスター [toranjisutā] = a transistor.

ウィンナーソーセージ [uinnā sōsēji] = a wiener or a Vienna sausage.

ゼミナール [zemināru] = a seminar; from German, also zemi and seminā.

ゼラチン [zerachin] = gelatin.

ゼラニウム [zeraniumu] = geranium(s).

ゼリー [zerii] = jelly.

ゼロ [zero] = one word for zero, 0.

ゼロックス [zerokkusu] = xerox copies or Xerox (brand name).

007 シリーズ [zero zero sebun shiriizu] = 007 series (movies, books).

ズボン [zubon] = trousers; from French jupon, petticoat.

PLACES

アジア [ajia] = Asia
アリゾナ [arizona] = Arizona
アルゼンチン [aruzenchin] = Argentina
バージニア [bājinia] = Virginia
ブラジル [burajiru] = Brazil
エジプト [ejip*u*to] = Egypt
カンボジア [kambojia] = Cambodia
ミズーリ [mizūri] = Missouri
ロサンゼルス [rosanzerus*u*] = Los Angeles (also ros*u*)
ルイジアナ [ruijiana] = Louisiana
サウジアラビア [saujiarabia] = Saudi Arabia
スエズ [suezu] = Suez
ウェールズ [uēruzu] = Wales

PEOPLE

ディズニー [dizunii] = Disney (also the beginning of dizuniirando)
エジソン [ejison] = Thomas Edison (other Edisons are エディソン).
エリザベス [erizabes*u*] = Elisabeth
ガンジー [ganjii] = Gandhi
ジーン [jiin] = Jean
ジム [jimu] = Jim
ジル [jiru] = Jill
クーリッジ [kūri(j)ji] = Coolidge (with a single or double j-sound)
スーザン [sūzan] = Susan
ウェルズ [ueruzu] = Wells

CHALLENGE

1. ゴジラ was created in 1954. His name comes from gorilla + kujira (whale). His English name is not a faithful translation of the katakana. What do we call him in English?
2. Which of the following words means buzzer, and which means bazaar? a) ブザー b) バザー
3. Many ways to order whiskey come from English. a) What does オンザロック come from? Do you remember these expressions from earlier lessons? b) ストレート c) シングル d) ダブル

4. In English, Asia is pronounced with /sh/ or /zh/; Brazil and Louisiana with /z/; Cambodia and Saudi Arabia with /d/; but all are spelled with ジ in katakana. Can you find the two countries listed in *PLACES* which are pronounced with /ji/ in Japanese *and* in English?

5. English -s is pronounced /s/ in blouse and loose, but /z/ in Wales, Blues and doubles. There is considerable confusion over s/z in Japanese. Only one of the following words has ス for an original /s/ and only one has ズ for an original /z/. Which words are they? a) doubles ダブルス b) Blues ブルーズ c) blouse ブラウス d) loose ルーズ e) Wales ウェールズ

ANSWERS

Practice:

school zone　スクールゾーン	jeans　ジーンズ
cheesecake　チーズケーキ	lasagna　ラザニア
rose wine　ロゼワイン	dessert　デザート
sausage　ソーセージ	studio　スタジオ

Challenge:

1. Godzilla. 2. a) buzzer b) bazaar 3. a) on the rocks b) straight c) a single d) a double 4. E*gy*pt and Vir*gi*nia 5. c) blouse has ス for /s/. e) Wales has ズ for /z/.

LESSON 16

ア	カ	サ	タ	ナ	ハ	**マ**		ラ	ワ
イ	キ	シ	チ	ニ	ヒ	ミ		リ	ン
ウ	ク	ス	ツ		フ	ム		ル	
エ	ケ	セ	テ	**ネ**	ヘ	メ		レ	
オ	コ	ソ	ト	**ノ**	ホ	**モ**		ロ	

NEW KANAS

Study how to pronounce the following kana and practice writing them.

ネ = ne, similar to the ne in net. This kana and ホ, ho, are the only kanas with more than three strokes.

ノ = no, similar but shorter than in no and nor. It is written with the same downward stroke as in ソ, so.

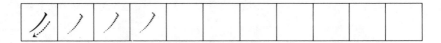

マ = ma, similar to the word ma. Try not to confuse it with ア, a.

モ = mo, similar but shorter than the mo's in most and more. It begins with the same two strokes as in テ, te.

RECOGNITION

The following kana are listed in Japanese alphabetical order.

Write the roman spellings for each of them.

イ＿　グ＿　コ＿　サ＿　ジ＿　ズ＿　チ＿　テ＿　ド＿　ナ＿

ニ＿　ネ＿　ノ＿　パ＿　ホ＿　マ＿　ミ＿　ム＿　メ＿　モ＿

ロ＿　ン＿

⟨ chi do gu ho i ji ko ma me mi mo ⟩
⟨ mu n/m na ne ni no pa ro sa te zu ⟩

When ン is followed by any m-kana it is pronounced m, never n, but some roman spelling systems spell it n.

KEY WORDS

Study the following key words, then practice writing them.

businessman
bi ji ne su
ビジネス

ma n
マン

"my home"
ma i hō mu
マイホーム

ammonia
a m mo ni a
アンモニア

The si in bu*si*nessman is spelled ジ, just like the si in tran*si*ster. A ビジネスホテル is a moderately-priced hotel for businessmen. The suffix マン is very popular in Japanese-English and is used in words like サラリーマン (a "salaried" man), and ガードマン (a "guard" man).

This actually means one's own home, so it could mean his home or her home or your home depending on the context. Two more examples with "my" are: マイペース, one's own pace; and マイカ -- one's privately owned car.

In English this word is pronounced with one m, but it has two m's in Japanese. The word comma (which is also pronounced with one m in English), can be spelled with one or two m's in Japanese: コマ or コンマ.

note(book)
nō to

ノート

This word is used instead of the longer word ノートブック to mean a notebook. When ノート is used with suru, it means to take notes. Once a note has been taken, however, it is more likely to be called a メモ than a ノート.

PRACTICE

Fill in ネ, ノ, マ and モ in the following words.

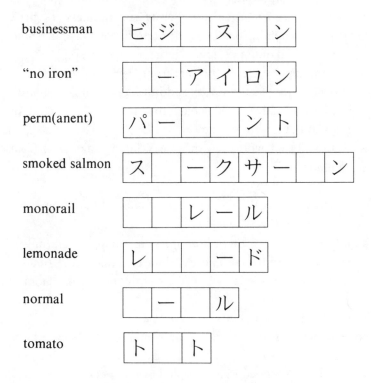

businessman	ビ	ジ		ス		ン	
"no iron"		ー	ア	イ	ロ	ン	
perm(anent)	パ	ー			ン	ト	
smoked salmon	ス		ー	ク	サ	ー		ン
monorail			レ	ー	ル		
lemonade	レ			ー	ド		
normal		ー		ル			
tomato	ト		ト				

NEW WORDS (including Key Words)

アンモニア [ammonia] = ammonia.

アーモンド [āmondo] = almonds or almond-flavored; sometimes amando.

アネモネ [anemone] = an anemone plant, not a sea anemone.

アラモード [a ra mōdo] = a la mode, topped with ice cream.

ビジネスホテル [bijinesu hoteru] = moderately-priced hotels which cater to traveling businessmen, but take tourists as well; probably from "business*man*" + "hotel".

ビジネスマン [bijinesuman] = a man in a better position than the average white-collar worker, a businessman.

ビジネスライク [bijinesuraiku] = businesslike; takes na.

ビジネススクール [bijinesu sukūru] = a business school.

ビジネスウーマン [bijinesuūman] = a businesswoman, not an average office worker; also bijinesugāru, "business" + "girl".

デモ [demo] = a marching demonstration; from demonsutorēshon.

エコノミーサイズ [ekonomii saizu] = large "economy-size".

エネルギー [enerugii] = energy, power; from German Energie.

ガードマン [gādoman] = a guard; the addition of "man" to "guard" is like the addition of "coat" to "blazer"—redundant in English but not in Japanese.

グラマー [guramā] = a woman with a sexy figure; takes na; from "glamor girl".

ハンマー [hammā] = a hammer.

ハーモニー [hāmonii] = Western concept of musical harmony.

ハネムーン [hanemūn] = a honeymoon.

ホモ [homo] = 1) shorter form of homojinaizu, homogenized (milk).
2) shorter form for homosekushuaru, homosexual (male).

ホームドラマ [hōmu dorama] = a T. V. soap opera; from "home" + "drama".

コマ [koma] or コンマ [komma] = a comma.

コネ [kone] = business or social connections; from konekushon.

クリスマス [kurisumasu] = December 25; a commercialized holiday, but not a public holiday, people have to work.

マチネー [machinē] = a matinee performance or show.

マダム [madamu] = proprietress of a bar; also mama.

マフィン [mafin] = an English muffin (a type of crumpet).

マフラー [mafurā] = 1) scarf-like muffler. 2) automotive muffler.

マーガリン [māgarin] = margarine; with a /ga/ not /ja/.

マイホーム [maihōmu] = one's own home; from "my" + "home".

マイカー [maikā] = one's own car.

マイク [maiku] = a mike, microphone.

マイクロフィルム [maikurofirumu] = microfilm.

マイペース [maipēsu] = one's own pace.

マジック [majikku] = a "magic" marker, a felt pen.

マジックテープ [majikku tēpu] = velcro self-fastening tape; from "magic" + "tape".

マージン [mājin] = a (typewriter's) margin.

マカロニウエスタン [makaroni uesutan] = a spaghetti Western; from "macaroni" + "Western".

ママ [mama] = 1) mom, mum. 2) proprietress of a bar; also madamu.

マーマレード [māmarēdo] = marmalade.

マネキン [manekin] = a display mannequin.

マニア [mania] = a mania, a craze.

マンツーマン [man tsū man] = one-on-one coaching or teaching (between males or females); from "man-to-man".

マラソン [marason] = a marathon race; with suru, to run a marathon.

マリネ [marine] = marinade or marinated; from French mariné.

マロン [maron] = chestnut-flavored or made with chestnuts; from French marron, chestnut.

マッサージ [massāji] = a Western massage; with suru, to give such a massage.

マスゲーム [masugēmu] = a group game; from "mass" + "game".

マスク [masuku] = a (gauze) mask.

マスメディア [masu media] = the mass media.

マスター [masutā] = 1) proprietor of a bar or similar establishment. 2) with キー, a master key. 3) with suru, to master a language or skill.

マッチ [matchi] = 1) matches. 2) with suru, to match clothes.

マトン [maton] = mutton.

メモ [memo] = a memo; with suru, to make a memo.

モダン [modan] = modern; takes na; also in words like modern

art, modan āto, and dance, modan dans*u*.

モデル [moderu] = a fashion model, model home, room, etc.

モカ [moka] = mocha, coffee-flavored.

モーニングコール [mōningu kōru] = a morning wake-up call in a hotel.

モーニングサービス [mōningu sābis*u*] = a morning time "set" which includes coffee or tea and usually two or more items such as: toast, roll, sandwich, salad, egg, and/or ham.

モノレール [monorēru] = monorail; the tōkyō monorēru goes to Haneda airport.

モルヒネ [moruhine] = morphine; from Dutch.

モルモット [morumotto] = a guinea pig or a marmot; perhaps from Dutch where both creatures bear the same name.

モットー [mottō] = a motto.

ネックレス [nekkures*u*] = a necklace.

ネクタイ [nek*u*tai] = necktie, also tai.

ネクタリン [nek*u*tarin] = a nectarine.

ネーム [nēmu] = one's name when it appears on personalized (engraved) belongings.

ネオンサイン [neon sain] = a neon sign.

ネル [neru] = flannel; this word was shortened from the front.

ネット [netto] = the type of net used in tennis and Ping-Pong (not for fishing); with suru, to net a ball.

ネットワーク [nettowāk*u*] = (T. V., transit) network.

ノーアイロン [nōairon] = permanent-press, wash-and-wear; from "no" + "iron".

ノーカーデー [nō kā dē] = a day when cars are not allowed in certain areas; from "no" + "car" + "day".

ノック [nokk*u*] = a knock, knocking; with suru, to knock on a door.

ノックアウト [nokkuauto] = a knockout, also K.O. (kē ō); with suru, to knockout.

ノーコメント [nō komento] = No comment! (popular response to reporters).

ノー・モア・ヒロシマ [nō moa hiroshima] = an anti-nuclear slogan; "no more" = never again; Hiroshima = Atomic-bomb destruction like that of Hiroshima.

ノンストップ [nons*u*topp*u*] = non-stop (elevator, train, plane).

ノルマ [noruma] = a norm, a standard; from Russian norma.

ノーマル [nōmaru] = normal type (hair, paper, etc.).

ノスタルジア [nos*u*tarujia] = nostalgia.

ノート [nōto] = 1) a notebook; rarely nōtobukk*u*. 2) reference notes; with suru, to make notes.

パーマ or パーマネント or パーマネントウェーブ [pāma/nento/ uēbu] = a perm, permanent, permanent wave; pāma is used the most.

ピアノ [piano] = the instrument or the musical notation, piano.

ピーマン [piiman] = small bell peppers; from French piment.

ポケットマネー [poketto manē] = pocket money.

レモン [remon] = lemon or lemon-flavored.

レモネード [remonēdo] = lemonade.

レモンティー [remontii] = tea with lemon, not milk; from "lemon" + "tea".

リモコン [rimokon] = 1) remote control; from rimōto kontorōru. 2) (husband) who goes home directly from work.

ロマンスグレー [romansu gurē] = a man with "romantically gray" hair.

サイドビジネス [saido bijines*u*] = a business on the side.

サーモン [sāmon] = one of several words for salmon, used in compounds like sāmon s*u*tēki (steaks) and sāmon pink*u* (pink).

サーモスタット [sāmos*u*tatto] = a thermostat.

サラリーマン [sarariiman] = a salaried male white-collar worker; from "salary" + "man".

シナモン [shinamon] = cinnamon or cinnamon-flavored.

スマート [sumāto] = smart only in the sense of stylish.

スモッグ [sumo(g)gu] = smog.

スモークサーモン [sumōk*u* sāmon] = smoked salmon.

スノーモービル [sunōmōbiru] = a snowmobile.

テーマ [tēma] = theme of a movie, a thesis, etc.; from German Thema.

テラマイシン [teramaishin] = Terramycin.

トマト [tomato] = tomato or tomato-flavored.

トンネル [tonneru] = train or automobile tunnel.

ワンマンカー [wamman kā] = a bus having one driver and no conductor (years ago female conductors were standard); from "one-man" + "car".

ゼネスト [zenes*u*to] = a general strike; from zeneraru s*u*toraiki.

PLACES

ベネズエラ [benezuera] = Venezuela

ハノイ [hanoi] = Hanoi

ホノルル [honoruru] = Honolulu

インドネシア [indoneshia] = Indonesia

マイアミ [maiami] = Miami

マニラ [manira] = Manila

マレーシア [marēshia] = Malaysia

モントリオール [montoriōru] = Montreal

モスクワ [mos*u*kuwa] = Moscow (from Russian Moskva)

ネパール [nepāru] = Nepal

ノバスコシア [noba s*u*koshia] = Nova Scotia

ノルマンディー [norumandii] = Normandy

ノルウェー [noruuē] = Norway

パナマ [panama] = Panama

ローマ [rōma] = Rome (from Italian Roma)

PEOPLE

アネット [anetto] = Annette

アーノルド [ānorudo] = Arnold

エレノア [erenoa] = Eleanor

ケネディ [kenedi] = Kennedy

マーガレット [māgaretto] = Margaret (also the marguerite flower)

マッカーサー [makkāsā] = MacArthur

マーク [māk*u*] = Mark (biblical Mark is maruko, from Portuguese)

マクドナルド [makudonarudo] = MacDonald (also MacDonald's restaurants)

マリア [maria] = Maria (also biblical Mary, from Portuguese)

モニカ [monika] = Monica

108

モリー [morii] ＝Molly
ネルソン [neruson] ＝Nelson
ノーマン [nōman] ＝Norman
セルマ [seruma] ＝Selma or Thelma
ティモシー [timoshii] ＝Timothy

CHALLENGE

1. What kind of computer do you think this is? マイコン
2. What kind of transmission would a ノークラッチ car have?
3. What kind of person is a ヘビースモーカー?
4. A film positive is a ポジ. What would a film negative be?
5. Daigaku means university. What do you think mas*u* puro daigaku means?

ANSWERS

Practice:

businessman ビジネスマン
"no iron" ノーアイロン
perm(anent) パーマネント
smoked salmon スモークサーモン

monorail モノレール
lemonade レモネード
normal ノーマル
tomato トマト

Challenge:

1. Both microcomputer and "my" computer are correct answers for maikon.
2. Nō kuratchi means automatic transmission, "no clutch".
3. A hebii sumōkā is a someone who smokes heavily.
4. ネガ (from ネガティブ).
5. Mass production of college graduates without quality education from a particular university.

LESSON 17

ア	カ	サ	タ	ナ	ハ	マ		ラ	ワ
イ	キ	シ	チ	ニ	ヒ	ミ		リ	ン
ウ	ク	ス	ツ	**ヌ**	フ	ム	**ユ**	ル	
エ	ケ	セ	テ	ネ	ヘ	メ		レ	
オ	コ	ソ	ト	ノ	ホ	モ		ロ	

NEW KANAS

Study how to pronounce the following kana and practice writing them.

ヌ =nu, shorter than the noo in noodle. Try not to confuse it with ス, su.

ユ =yu, shorter than the word you.

ニュ = nyu, shorter than the nu in menu. Though spelled ni+yu, the i-sound is not pronounced.

シュ =shu or sh$u$ (sh'). Similar to the shoo in shoot, but usually sh' when a k, t, p or a pause follows. Though spelled shi+ yu, neither i nor y is pronounced.

Any simple kana that begins with a consonant and ends with an i-sound can combine with a small yu like ni and shi do.

110

The following kanas lose their i's like ni+yu, nyu: ki+yu=kyu (*cu*pid); gi+yu=gyu (ar*gu*e); hi+yu=hyu (*Hu*ghes); pi+yu=pyu (*pu*pil); bi+yu=byu (tri*bu*te); mi+yu=(*mu*sic); and ri+yu=ryu (vo*lu*me).

When ji and chi combine with yu they lose both i and y, like shi+yu, shu: ji+yu=ju (*Ju*ne); chi+yu=chu (*chu*ewed).

Practice writing the following kanas.

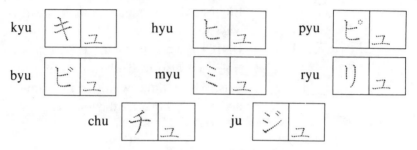

Many younger Japanese speakers are able to pronounce デュ as dyu and フュ as fyu. Older speakers, however, might pronounce デュ as deyu, and フュ as fuyu. These kana combinations are not very common.

RECOGNITION

The following kana are listed in Japanese alphabetical order. Write the roman spellings for each of them.

ウ＿ ギ＿ キュ＿ シ＿ シュ＿ ジュ＿ チ＿ チュ＿

ナ＿ ニ＿ ニュ＿ ヌ＿ ネ＿ ノ＿ ヒ＿ ヒュ＿ ビュ＿

ピュ＿ ミ＿ ミュ＿ ユ＿ リ＿ リュ＿ ワ＿

⟨ *byu chi chu gi hi hyu ju kyu mi myu na ne ni*
  no nu nyu pyu ri ryu shi shu u wa yu ⟩

ニュ, nyu is alphabetized under ニ, ni. It is alphabetized before ヌ, nu.

Hyu, pyu and byu are all alphabetized under ヒ, hi.

Some alternate roman spellings you might encounter are: tyu for chu, syu for shu, and zyu for ju.

KEY WORDS

UNESCO

yu ne s*u* ko

ユネスコ

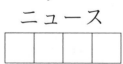

UNESCO is pronounced almost exactly the same way in Japanese as it is in English. But in Japanese there are two ways to spell it: ユネスコ or UNESCO. UNICEF (ユニセフ) and UFO (ユーフォー) are also read like words, not initials. These three words are all found under ユ in Japanese dictionaries.

minuet

me nu e t to

メヌエット

メヌエット comes from German Menuett. Foreign words spelled with ヌ are few, following is an almost exhaustive list: ヌードル (Western noodles); アンヌ (Anne, or any French name ending with -ne); ヌガー (nougat); and ヌード (nude). These words are easily outnumbered by those spelled with nyu, like menu: メニュー.

news

nyū s*u*

ニュース

Some English speakers say /nyūz/, others say /nūz/. In Japanese it is nyūs' and it is used by itself or in compounds like: テレビニュース, "T.V. news"; ホットニュース, "hot news"; ビッグニュース, "big news"; and ヒューイ・ルイス・アンド・ザ・ニュース, the group, Huey Lewis and the News.

flash

fu ra s sh*u*

フラッシュ

tuner

chū nā

チューナー

juice or deuce

jū s*u*

ジュース

Keep your eye out for this word, it is usually posted where flash photography is not permitted. Because シュ can become sh' you will find it at the end of most words which end with -sh in English. シュ is pronounced sh' in フラッシュキューブ, flash cube, because キューブ begins with a k-sound.

Some English speakers pronounce the "tu" in tuner /tu/ (like in *tu*ttifrutti), some pronounce it /chu/ (like in si*tua*-tion), but most people pronounce it /tyu/. Other words with チュ for /tyu/ include: チューブ (tube), スチュワーデス (stewardess), and シチュー (stew).

To most Japanese people, ジュース refers to carbonated fruit-flavored drinks. Occasionally it refers to real fruit juice, like in トマトジュース. Another meaning of ジュース is a tennis deuce. An original /dyu/ sound, as in deuce, sometimes becomes ju in Japanese.

PRACTICE

Fill in full-sized or half-sized ユ's in the following words.

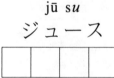

rush hour

ラ	ッ	シ		ア	ワ	ー

computer

コ	ン	ピ		ー	タ	ー

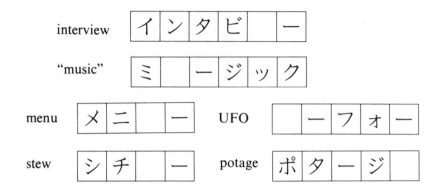

interview イ ン タ ビ 　 ー

"music" ミ 　 ー ジ ッ ク

menu メ ニ 　 ー

UFO 　 ー フ ォ ー

stew シ チ 　 ー

potage ポ タ ー ジ

NEW WORDS (including Key Words)

アイヌ [ainu] = the Caucasian Ainu people of Northern Japan; from the Ainu word for man.

ボリューム [boryūmu] = volume in the sense of a great quantity.

ビュッフェ [byuffe] = a buffet, especially in a train or train station.

ビューティフル [byūtifuru] = a stylish word for beautiful; takes na.

ビューティーサロン [byūtii saron] = one word for a beauty salon.

チューブ [chūbu] = a tube (tires, toothpaste, etc.).

チュチュ [chuchu] = a ballet tutu.

チューインガム [chūingamu] = chewing gum; also gamu.

チューナ [chūna] = canned tuna; also tsuna ツナ.

チューナー [chūnā] = (T. V., radio) tuner.

チューリップ [chūrippu] = a tulip.

デビュー [debyū] = a professional debut.

デュエット [d(e)yuetto] = a duet.

フィッシュサンド [fisshu sando] = a fried fish sandwich.

フォンデュ [fond(e)yu] = a fondue.

フラッシュ [furasshu] = news "flash" or photographic flash.

フラッシュキューブ [furasshu kyūbu] = a flash cube.

フレッシュ [furesshu] = fresh only in the sense of new, not old; takes na.

フューズ [f(u)yūzu] = an alternate, less popular spelling for hyūzu.

114

グレープフルーツジュース [grēp*u*frūtsu jūs*u*] = grapefruit-flavored soda or true grapefruit juice.

グレープジュース [grēpu jūs*u*] = grape-flavored soda or juice.

ヒューズ [hyūzu] = a fuse; occasionally spelled f(u)yūzu.

インタビュー [intabyū] = a T. V. or radio interview.

ジュース [jūs*u*] = 1) fruit-flavored soda or fruit juice. 2) tennis deuce; young people might say dyūs*u*.

カジュアル [kajuaru] = one of several words for casual (clothes, attitude).

カシューナッツ [kashūnatts*u*] = cashews; "nuts" is redundant in English, but not in Japanese.

コンピューター [kompyūtā] = a computer; often コン (kon) in compounds.

コミュニティー [komyunitii] = community in the sense of a social group.

キュロット [kyurotto] = culottes.

マニキュア [manikyua] = a manicure; with suru, to manicure.

マシュマロ [mashumaro] = marshmallows or marshmallow-flavored.

マッシュポテト [massh*u* poteto] = mashed potatoes.

マッシュルーム [masshurūmu] = Western-type mushrooms or mushroom-flavored.

メヌエット [menuetto] = a minuet; from German Menuett.

メニュー [menyū] = a menu.

ムードミュージック [mūdo myūjikk*u*] = music to relax to; from "mood" + "music".

ナチュラルチーズ [nachuraru chiizu] = unprocessed "natural" cheese.

ネームバリュー [nēmubaryū] = a name that carries prestige; from "name" + "value".

ヌード [nūdo] = nude.

ヌードル [nūdoru] = Western-style noodles.

ヌガー [nugā] = nougat confection; from French.

ニュアンス [nyuans*u*] = a nuance.

ニュース [nyūs*u*] = news.

ポピュラー [popyurā] = popular music; also popp*u* and popp*usu*.

ポタージュ [potāju] = any thick Western-style soup; from potage.

プッシュホン [pusshu̶hon] = a push-button phone.

ピューマ [pyūma] = a puma, cougar. mountain lion.

ピューレ [pyūre] = a puree.

ラッシュアワー [rasshuawā] = the rush hour(s).

レビュー [rebyū] = a theatrical revue.

レモンスカッシュ [remon s*u*kasshu] = carbonated lemonade, a lemon squash.

レーンシューズ or レインシューズ [rēnshūzu] = low waterproof boots; from "rain" + "shoes".

ルージュ [rūju] = 1) lipstick. 2) (cheek) rouge.

シチュー [shichū] or スチュー [s*u*chū] = a Western-style stew.

シュークリーム [shū kuriimu] = a cream puff; from "chou à la crème" + "cream".

シュノーケル [shunōkeru] = a snorkel; from the older spelling, schnorkel.

シュリンプサンド [shurimp*u* sando] = a fried shrimp sandwich.

シュート [shūto] = shooting a basketball or soccer ball; with suru, to shoot such a ball.

スチュワーデス [s*u*chuwādes*u*] = a stewardess.

スケジュール [s*u*kejūru] = one of several words for a schedule, program or plan.

トマトジュース [tomato jūs*u*] = tomato juice.

ユーフォー or U. F. O. [yūfō] = an unidentified flying object.

ユーモア [yūmoa] = humor, homorous.

ユネスコ or UNESCO [yunes*u*ko] = United Nations Educational, Scientific and Cultural Organization.

ユニホーム [yunihōmu] = a uniform worn by athletes (not a school or military uniform).

ユニーク [yūniik*u*] = one-of-a-kind, unique; takes na.

ユニセフ or UNICEF [yunisef*u*] = United Nations International Children's Emergency Fund.

ユニセックス [yunisekkusu] = unisex style.

ユニットバス [yunitto basu] = a prefabricated Western-style bathroom; from "unit" + "bath".

ユースホステル [yūsuhosuteru] = a youth hostel.

ユーターン or U-ターン [yūtān] = a U-turn; with suru, to make a U-turn.

ユーティリティールーム [yūtiritii rūmu] = a utility room.

ユートピア [yūtopia] = Utopia.

PLACES

バーミューダ [bāmyūda] = Bermuda

ブリティッシュ・コロンビア [buritisshu korombia] = British Colombia

チュニジア [chunijia] = Tunisia

ヒューストン [hyūsuton] = Houston

ジュネーブ [junēbu] = Geneva (from French Genève)

キューバ [kyūba] = Cuba

マサチューセッツ [masachūsettsu] = Massachusetts

ミュンヘン [myunhen] = Munich (from Geman München)

ニュージーランド [nyū jiirando] = New Zealand

ユーゴスラビア [yūgosurabia] = Yugoslavia

ユーコン [yūkon] = the Yukon

ユタ [yuta] = Utah

PEOPLE

アンヌ [annu] = Anne (after French pronunciation)

ドビュッシー [do byusshii] = Debussy

デュポン [d(e)yupon] = Du Pont

ヒューイ・ルイス [hyūi ruisu] = Huey Lewis

ジューン [jūn] = June

ジュニア or Jr. [junia] = Junior, as in Sammy Davis Jr.

ジュリエット [jurietto] = Juliet

マシュー [mashū] = Matthew (biblical Matthew is matai)

シューベルト [shūberuto] = Schubert (from German)

スチュアート [suchuāto] = Stuart

CHALLENGE

1. There are two ways to spell U-Boat in Japanese. What do you think they are?

2. Which of the following names a cocktail, which names a tool, and which names a small part?　a) スクリュー　b) ドライバー c) スクリュードライバー
3. A French "e" is often replaced with an u-kana. Find the one word below where this is *not* the case. a) アンヌ (Ann*e*) b) ポタージ ュ (potag*e*) c) ジュネーブ (Gen*è*v*e*) d) ドビュッシー (D*e*bussy) e) ルージュ (roug*e*) f) メートル (m*è*tr*e*)
4. Try to spell a) tuba and b) figure skate in katakana.
5. These are both ヒューイ・ルイス song titles from a record label printed in Japan. Can you translate these titles back into English? a) ユー・クラック・ミー・アップ b) アイ・ウォント・ア・ニ ュー・ドラッグ

ANSWERS

Practice:

rush hour	ラッシュアワー	menu	メニュー
computer	コンピューター	stew	シチュー
interview	インタビュー	UFO	ユーフォー
"music"	ミュージック	potage	ポタージュ

Challenge:

1. ユーボート or U-ボート.
2. a) screw＝a part b) (screw)driver＝a tool c) screwdriver＝a cocktail
3. French de, as in *De*bussy is usually spelled ド, do. (French du is spelled デュ, dyu, as in Du Pont.)
4. a) tuba＝チューバ b) figure skate＝フィギュアスケート (gyu is very rare in Japanese-English words)
5. a) yū ＊ kurakku ＊ mii ＊ app*u*＝You Crack Me Up b) ai ＊ uonto ＊ a ＊ nyū ＊ dora(g)gu＝I Want a New Drug

LESSON 18

ア	カ	サ	タ	ナ	ハ	マ	**ヤ**	ラ	ワ
イ	キ	シ	チ	ニ	ヒ	ミ	**ヰ**	リ	ン
ウ	ク	ス	ツ	ヌ	フ	ム	ユ	ル	
エ	ケ	セ	テ	ネ	ヘ	メ	**エ**	レ	
オ	コ	ソ	ト	ノ	ホ	モ	**ヨ**	ロ	

Y-KANAS

Japanese used to have five y-sounds: ya, yi, yu, ye, yo. Modern Japanese, however, uses only three of these sounds: ya, yu, and yo. The sounds yi and ye have become obsolete. Their kanas, ヰ and エ, have been replaced with イ, エ and イエ.

Ya and yo have full-sized forms and half-sized combining forms, like yu. Practice writing them.

ヤ = ya, similar to the ya in yard and the ia in Chianti. The first stroke is the same as in セ, se.

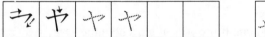

ヨ = yo, shorter than the yo's in yo-yo and York. This kana begins and ends like コ, ko.

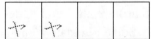

The most common combinations with a small ya are: kya (*Chia*nti); gya (*Guia*na); cha (*cha-cha-cha*); sha (*Sha*h); and ja (*Ja*va).

The most common combinations with a small yo are: cho (*cho*re); sho (*sho*re); and jo (*joy*).

Practice writing the following kanas.

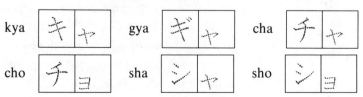

kya   gya   cha

cho   sha   sho

119

ja   ジャ   jo   ジョ

RECOGNITION

Circle all of the following kana that have an ah-sound. These are the key kanas used in Japanese alphabetizing and indexing.

イ	コ	サ	チ	ニ	ヘ	マ	ヨ	ロ	ン
ア	カ	シ	ツ	ナ	フ	モ	ヤ	ル	ワ
オ	キ	ス	タ	ノ	ハ	メ	ユ	ラ	

Words beginning with チ, chi, are found under the general category タ, ta. Words beginning with チャ (cha), then チュ (chu), then チョ (cho) are all found under チ.

Some alternate roman spellings you might encounter are: tya for cha, tyo for cho; sya for sha, syo for sho; and zya for ja, zyo for jo.

KEY WORDS

"hearing"

hi ya ri n gu

ヒヤリング

Earrings can be spelled either イヤリング or イアリング. ヒヤリング, however, is always spelled with ヤ. This word refers to an ability to listen and comprehend a foreign language, not to a general "hearing" ability.

"white shirt"

wa i sha ts*u*

ワイシャツ

ワイシャツ became Japanese at a time when all dress "shirts" were "white". Today it means a dress shirt of any color. An alternate spelling of this, probably patterned after T-shirt, is Y-シャツ.

120

catcher
kya t

キャッ

chā

チャー

Some other popular baseball terms include: ピッチャー (pitcher), and ショート (shortstop). キャ is often used to represent original ka-sounds like those in *ca*tcher and *ca*sh. (Likewise, ギャ is used in words like in *ga*llery, ギャラリー.)

"mansion"
ma n sho n

マンション

マンション does not refer to a large and impressive private house. It refers to a large and impressive apartment house or a flat in such a house. An apartment house which is not as tall or well-built as a マンション is called an アパート.

chocolate
cho ko

チョコ

rē to

レート

A common abbreviation of this word is チョコ. Many English speakers have difficulty pronouncing チョコレート correctly because it ends with *-rēto*, not *-rato*. This same long-a/short-a mix-up is responsible for the *-nē-* in マネージャー, ma*na*ger.

"jug"
jo k ki

ジョッキ

It is hard to see how this word came from jug, but apparently it did. In Japanese it refers to a large glass beer mug, the kind used at a ビヤガーデン (beer garden) or at a ビヤホール (beer hall).

PRACTICE

Fill in full-sized or half-sized ヤ's or ヨ's in the following words.

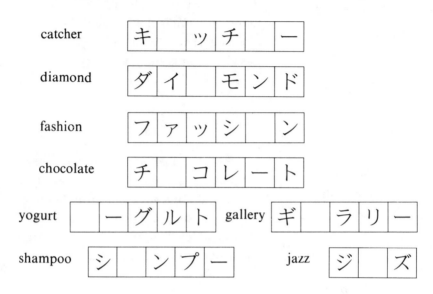

catcher　キ □ ッ チ □ ー

diamond　ダ イ □ モ ン ド

fashion　フ ァ ッ シ □ ン

chocolate　チ □ コ レ ー ト

yogurt　□ ー グ ル ト　gallery　ギ □ ラ リ ー

shampoo　シ □ ン プ ー　jazz　ジ □ ズ

NEW WORDS (including Key Words)

アダージョ [adājo] = adagio; also adājio.

アイシャドー [ai shadō] = eye shadow.

アイスキャンデー [aisu kyandē] = a popsicle, an ice-lolly; from "ice" + "candy".

ビヤガーデン [biya gāden] = a beer garden; also bia gāden.

ビヤホール [biya hōru] = a beer hall; also bia hōru.

ブイヨン [buiyon] = bouillon, broth.

ブラジャー [burajā] = a brassiere; originally burajiēru from French, when "Anglicized", -jiya (ジヤ) became -jā (ジャー).

チャック [chakku] = a fastener, a zipper; from the Japanese product name, "Chack".

チャーメン [chāmen] = chow mein (fried noodles); from Chinese chao mien.

122

チャームポイント [chāmu pointo] = an attractive physical feature such as one's mouth, legs, etc.; from "charm" + "point".

チャンネル [channeru] = a television channel.

チャンス [chans*u*] = a chance in the sense of an opportunity.

チャレンジ [charenji] = something challenging; with suru, to try something new or difficult.

チャーター [chātā] = chartered transportation; with suru, to charter transportation.

チャート [chāto] = a chart, diagram or graph.

チョッキ [chokki] = a vest; from Portuguese "jaque" or Dutch "jak".

チョコレート [chokorēto] = chocolate (candy) or chocolate-flavored; often shortened to choko in compounds.

チョーク [chōk*u*] = 1) chalk. 2) a choke for cars, motorcycles.

ダイヤ [daiya] = 1) a diamond in cards. 2) time scheduling for trains; from diaguramu, "diagram". 3) a diamond (gem); from daiyamondo.

ダイヤモンド [daiyamondo] = 1) a diamond (gem, not cards). 2) a baseball diamond.

デコレーションケーキ [dekorēshon kēki] = a store-bought cake with fancy icing; from "decoration" + "cake".

デリシャス [derishas*u*] = 1) delicious, tasty; takes na. 2) a Delicious (variety of American apple).

エシャロット [esharotto] = a shallot; from French échalote.

ファッション [fasshon] = fashion, mainly used in reference to clothes.

ファッションショー [fasshon shō] = a fashion show.

フィヨルド [fiyorudo] = a fjord, fiord.

ギヤ [giya] = gear(s).

ゴージャス [gōjas*u*] = wonderful, beautiful, gorgeous (clothes, buildings, food); takes na.

ゴージャスディナー [gōjasu dinā] = Such a beautiful dinner!; from "gorgeous" + "dinner".

グッドイヤー [guddoiyā] = Goodyear (the brand name).

ギャラ [gyara] = guaranteed remuneration for a model, singer, etc.; shortened from gyarantii, "guarantee".

ギャラリー [gyararii] = an art gallery.

ハイジャック [haijakku] = hijack, hijacking; with suru, to hijack.

ハイヤー [haiyā] = a hired car, a taxi that has been hired.

ハヤシライス [hayashi raisu] = beef stew served on rice; either from "hash" or the name "Hayashi" + "rice".

ヘヤドライヤー [heya doraiyā] = hair dryer; also hea doraiyā.

ヘヤコンディショナー [heya kondishonā] = hair conditioner.

ヒヤリング [hiyaringu] = listening comprehension ability of a foreign language; from "hearing".

イミテーション [imitēshon] = something fake, an imitation.

イヤホン [iyahon] = an earphone; also iahon.

イヤリング [iyaringu] = 1) earring(s). 2) a yearling.

ジャケット [jaketto] = a jacket (coat or record sleeve); also jaketsu.

ジャンボ [jambo] = jumbo-sized.

ジャンパー [jampā] = jumper in the sense of a jacket; also jambā.

ジャンプ [jampu] = a jump (especially in sports); with suru, to make a jump.

ジャム [jamu] = jam (preserves).

ジャーナリスト [jānarisuto] = a journalist.

ジャル or JAL [jaru] = Japan Airlines, J. A. L.

ジャズ [jazu] = jazz music.

ジンジャー [jinjā] = the spice ginger or ginger-flavored, not ginger root.

ジョギング [jogingu] = jogging; with suru, to jog; with shūzu, running shoes.

ジョッキ [jokki] = large glass beer mug; from jug.

ケチャップ [kechappu] = ketchup, catsup.

コマーシャルソング [komāsharu songu] = a jingle or song used to advertise; from "commercial" + "song".

コミュニケーション [komyunikēshon] = communication (implies communication between equals not between superiors and inferiors).

コニャック [konyakku] = cognac; ni + ya = nya.

コレクション [korekushon] = a collection of new fashions, records, stamps, etc.

クッション [kusshon] = sofa or chair cushions (not Japanese floor cushions).

キャバレー [kyabarē] = a cabaret with "hostesses", a dance band and sometimes a floor show.

キャベツ [kyabetsu] = Western cabbage (not Chinese cabbage).

キャディー [kyadii] = a golf caddy; with suru, to caddy.

キャンペーン [kyampēn] = commercial campaigning; with suru, to run a (sales) campaign.

キャンプ [kyampu] = 1) recreational camping; with suru, to camp out. 2) pro baseball spring training camps; from supuringu kyampu.

キャノン [kyanon] = Canon (the brand name).

キャンセル [kyanseru] = a cancellation in a schedule; with suru, to cancel something scheduled.

キャンティ [kyanti] = Chianti (wine).

キャセロール [kyaserōru] = a casserole.

キャッシュ [kyasshu] = cash, not credit.

キャッシュカードコーナー [kyasshu kādo kōnā] = area in a bank where the cash-dispensing machines are located; from "cash-card" + "corner".

キャッチャー [kyatchā] = a baseball catcher; more popular than the non-loan word hoshu (hoshu is a direct translation of catcher: ho = "catch", shu = "-er").

キャッチボール [kyatchi bōru] = a game of catch with a baseball; with suru, to play catch; "ball" is redundant in English, but not in Japanese.

マネージャー [manējā] = a manager of sports teams, talent, hotels, etc.

マンション [manshon] = a high-rise modern apartment building.

マヨネーズ [mayonēzu] = mayonnaise; from French.

ナイスショット [naisu shotto] = Nice shot! (golf); shotto is a golf term, shūto (shoot) is used in games like soccer and basketball, but not in golf.

ナショナル [nashonaru] = National (the brand name).

ノンフィクション [nonfik*u*shon] = non-fiction.

オイルショック [oiru shokk*u*] = the oil crisis; from "oil" + "shock".

パジャマ [pajama] = pajamas.

ポークジンジャー [pōku jinjā] = pork sauted in ginger.

ラムチョップ [ramu chopp*u*] = lamb chops (cooked or ready-to-cook).

レジャーウェア [rejā uea] = leisure wear.

レーヨン [rēyon] = rayon.

ロードショー [rōdo shō] = a first-run "show" (movie or premiere) that will later go on the "road" to cheaper theaters.

ローション [rōshon] = lotion.

シャーベット [shābetto] = sherbet.

シャンプー [shampū] = shampoo.

シャンソン [shanson] = a chanson, a song; from French.

シャープ [shāpu] = 1) the brand name, Sharp. 2) sharp; takes na. 3) a musical sharp (♯).

シャープペンシル or シャープペン [shāp*u* pen/shiru] = a mechanical pencil; from "Ever*sharp*", creators of mechanical pencils.

シャツ [shats*u*] = an undershirt; from "shirt".

シャワー [shawā] = a bathroom shower.

ショコラ [shokora] = an alternate word for chocolate used in some French desserts; from French chocolat.

ショート [shōto] = 1) a short circuit; with suru, to short-circuit. 2) a shortstop; also shōtos*u*topp*u*.

ショートケーキ [shōtokēki] = shortcake.

スペシャル [s*u*pesharu] = a special sale, feature, etc.

タイヤ [taiya] = a tire, tyre.

トヨタ [toyota] = Toyota (the brand name).

ワイシャツ or Y-シャツ [waishats*u*] = a dress shirt of any color; from "white" + "shirt"; this begins wai, not howai(to), because it comes from *spoken* American English.

ヤマハ [yamaha] = Yamaha (the brand name).

ヤング [yangu] = a modern word for young people.

ヨードチンキ [yōdochinki] = tincture of iodine; from German Jodtinktur.

ヨーグルト [yōguruto] = yogurt.

ヨーグルトドリンク [yōguruto dorink*u*] = drinkable yogurt.

ヨット [yotto] = a small sailboat, not a luxury liner; from British English "yacht".

PLACES

チャド [chado] = Chad
ヒマラヤ [himaraya] = the Himalayas
ジャカルタ [jakaruta] = Jakarta
ジャワ [jawa] = Java
ジョージア [jōjia] = Georgia
ニュージャージー [nyū jājii] = New Jersey
ニューヨーク [nyū yōk*u*] = New York
ワルシャワ [warushawa] = Warsaw (from Warszawa)
ヨハネスバーグ [yohanesubāgu] = Johannesburg
ヨークシャー [yōk*u*shā] = Yorkshire
ヨーロッパ [yōroppa] = Europe (from Dutch Europa)
ヨルダン [yorudan] = Jordan

PEOPLE

チャイコフスキー [chaikof*u*skii] = Tchaikovsky
チャールズ [chāruzu] = Charles (for a Frenchman, シャルル)
チョーサー [chōsā] = Chaucer
ジャック [jakk*u*] = Jack
ジョエル [joeru] = Joel
ジョイス [jois*u*] = Joyce
ジョン [jon] = John (Biblical John is ヨハネ)
ジョーン [jōn] = Joan
ジョセフ [josef*u*] = Joseph (for a German, ヨセフ)
キャレン [kyaren] = Caren, Karen (can also be karen)
キャロル [kyaroru] = Carroll, Carol (can also be karoru)
リチャード [richādo] = Richard
シャーロット [shārotto] = Charlotte
ショーン [shōn] = Sean
ヨハン・セバスチャン・バッハ [yohan sebas*u*chan bahha] = Johann Sebastian Bach

CHALLENGE

1. Yebisu beer is often spelled with the old kana for ye: エビス. How do you think Yebisu is pronounced in Japanese?
2. What longer words do you think combined to make these words?
a) チョコピー (a sweet snack)   b) マスコミ (mass media).
3. Chinese-style fried rice is chāhan. Chāmen (chow mein) is fried noodles. Gyōza are stuffed dumplings and shūmai are stuffed pastries. These are katakana words, can you spell them? a) chāhan b) chāmen c) gyōza d) shūmai
4. These two things are both found in a car. What are they? a) トランスミッション b) キャブレター
5. Road show, decoration cake, ice candy, catch ball, charm point and Chack are a few examples of ジャパニーズイングリッシュ. What is ジャパニーズイングリッシュ?

ANSWERS

Practice:

catcher キャッチャー	yogurt ヨーグルト
diamond ダイヤモンド	shampoo シャンプー
fashion ファッション	gallery ギャラリー
chocolate チョコレート	jazz ジャズ

Challenge:

1. エビス is pronounced e-bi-s*u*. (Just like in yen, ye=e.)
2. a) chokopii = chokorēto piinatts*u* (chocolate-covered peanuts).
b) mas*u* komi = mas*u* komyunikēshon (mass communication).
3. a) chāhan=チャーハン   b) chāmen=チャーメン   c) gyōza= ギョーザ   d) shūmai=シューマイ
4. a) a transmission b) a carburetor
5. japaniizu ingurissh*u*= "Japanese English": New words made in Japan using English parts. These words are used in standard written and spoken Japanese. Often they are used by Japanese people in spoken and written English, unaware that they are not using standard English.

LESSON 19

ア	カ	サ	タ	ナ	ハ	マ	ヤ	ラ	ワ
イ	キ	シ	チ	ニ	ヒ	ミ	(ヰ)	リ	ン
ウ	ク	ス	ツ	ヌ	フ	ム	ユ	ル	
エ	ケ	セ	テ	ネ	ヘ	メ	(ヱ)	レ	
オ	コ	ソ	ト	ノ	ホ	モ	ヨ	ロ	

NEW KANAS, NEW SOUNDS

These kana combinations are not native to the Japanese language, but are not difficult for Japanese people to pronounce. Practice writing them.

チェ = che, similar to the che in chess. Though spelled chi+e, the i is not pronounced.

シェ = she, similar to the she in sherry.

ジェ = je, similar to the je in jet.

ツァ = tsa, similar to the za in Mozart.

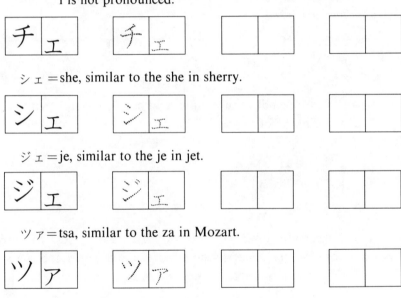

NEW KANAS, CONFUSED SOUNDS

Most Japanese people can pronounce these sounds easily, even though they are not native Japanese sounds: fa, fi, fe, fo; ti, di; and che, she, je, tsa.

The following sounds are not easy for all Japanese people to pronounce: fyu, dyu, du, tu and vu. These sounds all have alternate easier-to-pronounce pronunciations. The pronunciations for デュ and フュ are dyu/deyu, and fyu/fuyu. Study the spelling and alternate pronunciations for tu, du and vu.

トゥ = tu or tou, most speakers pronounce this almost like the word tow, but some people are able to pronounce this like the tu in tutti.

ドゥ = du or dou, usually resembles the word doe more than the last half of voodoo.

ヴ = vu or bu, resembles the beginning of boo-hoo more often than the beginning of voodoo. This kana is half u (ウ), half bu (ブ).

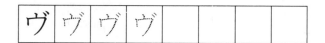

By adding small vowels to ヴ, "va", "vi", "ve" and "vo" are created. The u-sound is not pronounced in these words and the v-sound is more like a b-sound for most speakers.

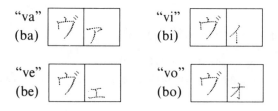

"va" (ba)   "vi" (bi)

"ve" (be)   "vo" (bo)

RECOGNITION

Only four of the sounds written below in roman spelling are also used in native Japanese words: fu, bu, u, wa. The sounds below are listed in Japanese alphabetical order. Write the katakana spellings for each of them.

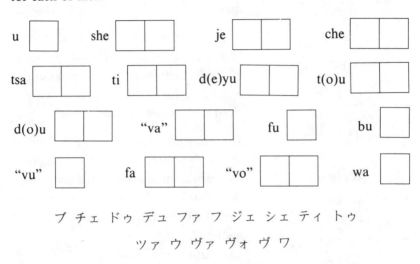

u ☐　　she ☐☐　　je ☐☐　　che ☐☐

tsa ☐☐　　ti ☐☐　　d(e)yu ☐☐　　t(o)u ☐☐

d(o)u ☐☐　　"va" ☐☐　　fu ☐　　bu ☐

"vu" ☐　　fa ☐☐　　"vo" ☐☐　　wa ☐

ブ チェ ドゥ デュ ファ フ ジェ シェ ティ トゥ
ツァ ウ ヴァ ヴォ ヴ ワ

All words spelled with ヴ have alternate spellings with バ, ビ, ブ, ベ or ボ. They are usually alphabetized as if they were spelled with バ, ビ, ブ, ベ or ボ, but occasionally they are alphabetized under ウ, u.

KEY WORDS

"image change"

i me che n

イ メ チェ ン

☐☐☐☐☐

Both this word and the full form イメージチェンジ mean a change in appearance or image. When used with suru they mean to change a personal or corporate image.

131

shake

shē k*u*

シェーク

A ミルクセーキ is an original Japanese drink made of milk and egg that just barely resembles an American milk shake. A シェーク on the other hand is usually an authentic American-style milk shake.

jet *"aircraft"*

je t to *"ki"*

ジェット機

				機

ジェット by itself is short for a jet engine, ジェットエンジン, not a jet plane. A jet plane is jettoki (機,ki, means aircraft). A ジェットコースター is a popular word for a roller coaster.

Wagner

"va" gu nā

ヴァグナー

The standard spelling of this German composer's name is ワグナー (wagunā), but music publishers often prefer the more "authentic" v-spelling: ヴァグナー. *Viva*ldi and Beetho*v*en also have standard spellings: ビバルディ, ベートーベン, and "authentic" spellings: ヴィヴァルディ, ベートーヴェン. Mozart has only one spelling: モーツァルト.

PRACTICE

To each English spelling, match the two Japanese spellings.

チェロ ●	● pizza ●	● ミルクセーキ
ピッツァ ●	● gesture ●	● ビバルディ
ミルクシェーク ●	● cello ●	● セロ
クリスマスイヴ ●	● Vivaldi ●	● ツッティ
ジェスチャー ●	● milk shake ●	● ピザ
トゥッティ ●	● X-mas Eve ●	● ゼスチュア
ヴィヴァルディ ●	● tutti ●	● クリスマスイブ

132

NEW WORDS

アバンギャルド or アヴァンギャルド [aban gyarudo] = avant-garde.

アールヌーボー or アールヌーヴォー [āru nūbō] = art nouveau.

バイオリン or ヴァイオリン [baiorin] or ヴィオリン [biorin] = violin.

ビオラ or ヴィオラ [biora] = viola.

ボーカル or ヴォーカル [bōkaru] = vocals.

ブードゥー [būd(o)ū] = voodoo.

チェダーチーズ [chedā chiizu] = cheddar cheese.

チェック [chekku] = 1) checked pattern. 2) an inspection; with suru, to inspect or check out a problem. 3) a bank check.

チェックアウト [chekku auto] = checking out of a hotel; with suru, to check out.

チェックイン [chekku in] = checking into a hotel; with suru, to check in.

チェーン [chēn] = tire chains; also taiya chēn. 2) franchised, chain stores; also chēn sutoa.

チェンジコート [chenjikōto] = changing ends; with suru, to change ends; from "change" + "court".

チェリー [cherii] = cherry-flavored, as in cherii burandē, cherry brandy.

チェロ [chero] = cello; also sero.

チェス [chesu] = a game of chess; with suru, to play chess.

ダイジェスト [daijesuto] = digest in the sense of a condensed review, usually of sports.

イメチェン [ime chen] = a change in image; also imēji chenji; with suru, to change one's image; from "image" + "change".

インターチェンジ [intāchenji] = a highway interchange.

ジェネレーション [jenerēshon] = a modern word for generation.

ジェリービーンズ [jerii biinzu] = jelly beans; also zerii biinzu.

ジェスチャー [jesuchā] = a gesture; with suru, to gesture, to gesticulate; also zesuchā and zesuchua.

ジェトロ or JETRO [jetoro] = JETRO, Japan External Trade Organization.

ジェットエンジン [jetto enjin] = a jet engine; also jetto.

ジェット機 [jetto ki] = a jet airplane; from "jet" + "aircraft".

ジェットコースター [jetto kōsutā] = a roller coaster; from "jet" + "coaster".

コンチェルト [koncheruto] = a concerto.

クリスマスイヴ [kurisumasu ibu] = Christmas Eve; also ibu.

モッツァレラチーズ [mottsarera chiizu] = mozzarella cheese.

ネグリジェ [negurije] = women's negligee.

オクターブ or オクターヴ [okutābu] = an octave.

ピッツァ [pittsa] = pizza; also piza.

ランジェリー [ranjerii] = women's lingerie; from French.

シェア [shea] = a share, shea 20 pāsento = 20% share.

シェフ [shefu] = a chef.

シェーク or シェイク [shēku] = an American-style milk shake; also mirukushēku.

シェパード [shepādo] = a German shepard, an Alsatian; also sepādo.

シェイプアップ [sheipu appu] = working out and shaping up; with suru, to shape up one's body.

シェリー [sherii] = sherry.

トゥエンティワン [t(o)uentiwan] = the card game 21.

トゥッティ [t(o)utti] = the musical term tutti; also tsutti.

ツァー [tsā] = a Russian tsar, czar.

PLACES

アルジェリア [arujeria] = Algeria

チェコ or チェコスロバキア [cheko/surobakia] = Czechoslovakia, Czech

マンチェスター [manchesutā] = Manchester

ナイジェリア [naijeria] = Nigeria

セイシェル [seisheru] = the Seychelles

シェットランド [shettorando] = Shetland (ウール, wool or ポニー, pony)

PEOPLE

バネッサ or ヴァネッサ [banessa] = Vanessa

ベルマ or ヴェルマ [beruma] = Velma

ベートーベン or ベートーヴェン [bētōben] = Beethoven
ビバルディ or ヴィヴァルディ [bibarudi] = Vivaldi
ドボルザーク or ドヴォルザーク [doboruzāku] = Dvořak
フィッツジェラルド [fittsujerarudo] = Fitzgerald
イボン or イヴォン [ibon] = Yvonne
イブ or イヴ [ibu] = Eve
ジェフ [jefu] = Jeff
ジェニファー [jenifā] = Jennifer
ミシェル [misheru] = Michelle
モーツァルト [mōtsaruto] = Mozart
ピュリッツァー [pyurittsā] = Pulitzer
ラベル or ラヴェル [raberu] = Ravel
レーチェル [rēcheru] = Rachel
シェークスピア [shēkusupia] = Shakespeare
ワグナー [wagunā] or ヴァグナー [bagunā] = Wagner (Wilhelm Richard)

CHALLENGE

All katakana characters are adaptations of Chinese characters. katakana ki, キ, can be traced to the right half of the character ki, 幾, in jettoki, ジェット機.

A second generation Japanese is called a nisei. Compare how this is written in Chinese characters, 二世, and in katakana, ニセイ.

The following words are spelled three ways. All of these words are found in place names and/or addresses. Try to match the less common katakana and roman spellings to their standard Japanese-Chinese character spellings.

nichōme ●   ● ミタ   ●   ● 江戸
hatchōme ●   ● チバ   ●   ● 八丁目
Edo ●   ● エド   ●   ● 二丁目
Mita ●   ● ニチョウメ   ●   ● 三田
Chiba ●   ● ハッチョウメ ●   ● 千葉

135

ANSWERS

Practice:

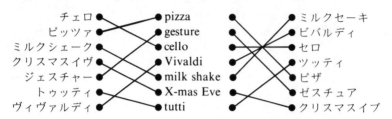

Challenge:

LESSON 20

ア	カ	サ	タ	ナ	ハ	マ	ヤ	ラ	ワ
イ	キ	シ	チ	ニ	ヒ	ミ	(ヰ)	リ	ン
ウ	ク	ス	ツ	ヌ	フ	ム		ユ	ル
エ	ケ	セ	テ	ネ	ヘ	メ	(ヱ)		レ
オ	コ	ソ	ト	ノ	ホ	モ		ヨ	ロ

JAPANESE PARTICLES

Japanese particles, like most native Japanese words, are rarely written in katakana. When the particles wa, e and o are written in katakana, they are not spelled ワ, エ and オ. Study how they are written and practice writing them.

ハ = wa. This is spelled like ha.

ヘ = e. This is spelled like he.

ヲ = o.　An older pronunciation of this is wo. Write one horizontal bar, then another shorter one, then add ノ, no.

RECOGNITION

Write the roman spelling for each of the following Japanese particles.

ガ__　　ト__　　ニ__　　ハ__　　ヘ__　　モ__　　ヲ__

⟨e ga mo ni to wa (w)o⟩

137

THE JAPANESE-ENGLISH ALPHABET

The Japanese alphabet (アルファベット) is based on the English version of the Roman alphabet. Not all of the letters have predictable Japanese pronunciations.

Because Japanese people have so much trouble differentiating B and V, "bui" was created. Bui is spelled ブイ or ヴィ or V. Beverly spelled outloud in Japanese is: bii-ii-bui-ii-āru-eru-wai.

Japanese Z is pronounced zetto. This comes from British zed. American pronunciation of Z, /zii/, should be avoided because Japanese speakers easily confuse it with G, /jii/. Fitzgerald spelled outloud is: ef*u*-ai-tii-zetto-jii-ii-āru-ē-eru-dii.

Before the ティ / ディ spelling innovation, T was spelled テ― (tē) and D was spelled デ― (dē). Some older people still use these pronunciations, so it is possible you could hear Fitzgerald spelled with tē and dē instead of tii and dii.

Letters of the Japanese-English alphabet are not usually alphabetized A-B-C, but アイウエオ. REO Speedwagon records would be found at the very beginning of a group of records under ア (for āru-ii-ō), not under a non-existent "R".

You might sometimes be asked to spell out your name at the cleaners or photo shop or over the telephone. Study how to pronounce the letters below to ensure your being understood.

A エ― (ē)	J ジェ― (jē)	T ティ― (tii)
B ビ― (bii)	K ケ― (kē)	or テ― (tē)
C シ― (shii)	L エル (eru)	U ユ― (yū)
D ディ― (dii)	M エム (emu)	V ブイ or ヴィ (bui)
or デ― (dē)	N エヌ (enu)	W タブリュ― (daburyū)
E イ― (ii)	O オ― (ō)	X エックス (ekk*us*u)
F エフ (ef*u*)	P ピ― (pii)	Y ワイ (wai)
G ジ― (jii)	Q キュ― (kyū)	Z ゼット (zetto)
H エッチ (etchi)	R アール (āru)	
I アイ (ai)	S エス (es*u*)	

NEW WORDS—LETTERS AND SYMBOLS

IBM [ai bii emu] = IBM, International Business Machines.

RCA [āru shii ē] = RCA, Radio Corporation of America.

BBC [bii bii shii] = British Broadcasting Corporation.

VIP [bui ai pii] = VIP, very important person; also bipp*u*.

VSOP [bui esu ō pii] = Very Superior Old Pale (brandy).

V-ネックセーター [bui nekk*u*sētā] = a V-necked sweater.

VOA [bui ō ē] = VOA, Voice of America (short-wave broadcast).

V-サイン [bui sain] = V for Victory sign.

DJ [dii jē] = a DJ, also dis*u*ku jokkii.

DK [dii kē or dē kē] = kitchen with a dining area; also dainingu-kitchin.

$ [doru] = dollar (s).

へ [e] = the Japanese particle e.

ABC [ē bii shii] = 1) the basics, the ABC's of something. 2) the American Broadcasting Company. 3) the Australian Broadcasting Commission.

AM [ē emu] = 1) AM (radio), amplitude modulation; also MW in Japan. 2) AM, ante meridiem; often *precedes* the hour: AM 8 = 8 AM.

FBI [efu bii ai] = the FBI, Federal Bureau of Investigation.

FM [efu emu] = FM (radio), frequency modulation.

X-線 [ekk*usu* sen] = X-ray; from "X"+"line"; also rentogen, after the inventor Röntgen.

MVP [emu bui pii] = MVP, most valuable player.

MW [emu daburyū] = Medium Wave, same as AM (radio).

¥ [en] = yen.

NHK [enu etchi kē] = NHK, Nihon Hōso Kyōkai (the Japanese Broadcasting Company).

NG [enu jii] = the scene or shot is "no good" (so do it again).

LP [eru pii] = LP, long-playing (record).

SF [esu ef*u*] = Sci-Fi, SF, science fiction.

HB [etchi bii] = "hard black" pencil lead.

EEC [ii ii shii] = the European Economic Community; the European Common Market.

JVC [jē bui shii] = the Japan Victor Company, more commonly known as bik*u*tā in Japan.

JTB [jē tii bii] = the Japan Travel Bureau.

GNP [jii enu pii] = the GNP, gross national product.

－ドライバー [mainasu doraibā] = a flat-headed screwdriver; from the "minus sign" shape of the blade.

ヲ [o or wo] = the Japanese particle o (wo).

OB [ō bii] = former (male) classmates or club members; from "old boy".

OA [ō ē] = office automation; also ofisu ōtomēshon.

OL [ō eru] = a female office worker; from "office"+"lady".

OG [ō jii] = former female classmates or club members; from "old girl".

OK [ō kē or okkē] = OK; not used as much in Japan as in other countries.

PR [pii āru] = PR, public relations; with suru, to publicize.

PM [pii emu] = PM, post meridiem; PM 8 = 8 PM.

PTA [pii tii ē] = the PTA, Parent Teacher Associations (in Japan).

£ [pondo] = pound sterling.

＋ドライバー [purasu doraibā] = a Phillips screwdriver; from the "plus sign" shape of the blades.

CIA [shii ai ē] = the CIA, Central Intelligence Agency.

CM [shii emu] = a commercial; from "commercial message".

CC [shii shii] = a cc, a cubic centimeter.

ハ [wa] = the Japanese particle wa.

YWCA [wai daburyū shii ē] = the YWCA, Young Women's Christian Association (in Japan).

YMCA [wai emu shii ē] = the YMCA, Young Men's Christian Association (in Japan).

UPI [yū pii ai] = the UPI, United Press International.

COMPREHENSIVE REVIEW (Lessons 1-20)

ALPHABETIZING

I. Katakana syllabary charts should be read: **a,** i, u, e, o; **ka,** ki, ku, ke, ko; **sa,** shi, su, se, so; etc. Fill in the missing kana and roman letters in the following charts.

ア	カ	サ		ナ		マ			ワ
イ		シ	チ		ヒ	ミ	ヰ	リ	
	ク		ツ	ヌ	フ		ユ		
エ		セ		ネ			ヱ	レ	
	コ		ト		ホ	モ			

a		ta	ha		ra
ki		ni		yi	n/m
u	su		mu	ru	
ke	te	he	ye		
o	so	no		yo	

II. Circle the kana or letter in each of the following groups that would come first if alphabetized Japanese-style.

EXAMPLES: ソ リ ツ ㋕ (za [sa+ ゛] comes first, then so, tsu, ri)

Ⓝ O P Q (enu comes first, then ō, kyū, pii [hi+ ゜])

1. マ ヤ ア セ	3. モ テ キ ニ	5. Q R S T
2. ナ ラ ホ オ	4. A B C D	6. W X Y Z

KANA CONVERSION

Convert the following kanas into different kanas by adding one stroke. EXAMPLE: fu → nu means convert フ into ヌ, do this by adding ＼ to フ : ヌ.

1. fu→su フ	4. wa→u ワ	7. ku→ta ク	10. so→tsu ソ
2. n→shi ン	5. ko→yo コ	8. no→me ノ	11. ri→sa リ
3. re→ru レ	6. na→chi ナ	9. no→so ノ	12. ko→ro コ

141

KATAKANA CROSSWORDS

I. This crossword puzzle is made up of names of Japanese drinks. Fill in the names using kana, then check your answers against the key. Half-sized kanas and dashes have already been filled in.

DOWN

1 coffee float
2 cocoa
3 lemon squash
4 yogurt drink
7 Japanese-style milk shake
10 wine

ACROSS

1 Coca-Cola
5 grapefruit soda or juice
6 beer
8 hot milk
9 tea with lemon
11 whiskey

II. This puzzle contains only names of major cities. Translate these names into English and check your answers with the key.

DOWN	ACROSS
1 _____	2 _____
3 _____	6 _____
4 _____	7 _____
5 _____	9 _____
8 _____	11 _____
10 _____	13 _____
12 _____	

Grid:

- 1 (down): ロ
- 2 (across): サ ン ³フ ラ ン ⁴シ ス コ   ⁵バ
- ⁶ウ ィ ー ン | ラ | ド | ン
- ゼ | ン | ⁷ニ ュ ー ⁸ヨ ー ク
- ⁹ホ ノ ル ル | ク | ｜ | ハ | ｜
- ス | フ | ネ | バ
- ル | ¹⁰ロ | ス | ｜
- ¹¹ト ロ ン ト | バ
- ¹²パ | ド | ｜
- ¹³ウ エ リ ン ト ン | グ

143

KANA FROM KANJI

Chinese characters, like 幾, are called kanji. Katakana ki, キ, comes from the printed version of the kanji ki, 幾. Hiragana ki, き, comes from cursive version of ki, 幾. When compared to each other, katakana looks block-like and hiragana looks more cursive.

Below are some katakana and hiragana symbols next to the kanjis they originated from. Use rōmaji (roman letters) to write the sounds each set has in common.

sound	katakana	kanji block	cursive	hiragana		sound	katakana	kanji block	cursive	hiragana
____	キ	幾	幾	き		____	カ	加	加	か
____	リ	利	利	り		____	ロ	呂	呂	ろ
____	コ	己	己	こ		____	ソ	曽	曽	そ
____	モ	毛	毛	も		____	ホ	保	保	ほ
____	ウ	宇	宇	う		____	ナ	奈	奈	な
____	セ	世	世	せ		____	ユ	由	由	ゆ
____	ヤ	也	也	や		____	メ	女	女	め
____	ク	久	久	く		____	ヌ	奴	奴	ぬ
____	ヨ	与	与	よ		____	ネ	祢	祢	ね
____	テ	天	天	て		____	レ	礼	礼	れ

ANSWERS FOR COMPREHENSIVE REVIEW
ALPHABETIZING

I. See Appendix A for filled-in charts.

II.

1. ア (a) then se, ma, ya
2. オ (o) then na, ho, ra
3. キ (ki) then te, ni, mo
4. A (ē) then shii, dii, bii
5. R (āru) then es*u*, kyū, tii
6. X (ekk*usu*) then zetto, daburyū, wai

KANA CONVERSION

1. フ→ス 2. ン→シ 3. レ→ル 4. ワ→ウ 5. コ→ヨ 6. ナ→チ 7. ク→タ 8. ノ→メ 9. ノ→ソ 10. ソ→ツ 11. リ→サ 12. コ→ロ

KATAKANA CROSSWORDS

I.

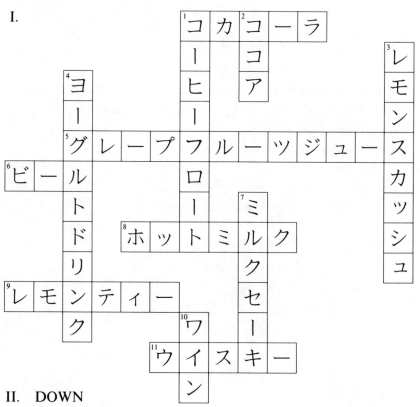

II. DOWN
1 Los Angeles
3 Frankfurt
4 Sidney
5 Vancouver
8 Johannesburg
10 London
12 Paris

ACROSS
2 San Francisco
6 Vienna
7 New York
9 Honolulu
11 Toronto
13 Wellington

KANA FROM KANJI

ki (キ), ri (リ), ko (コ), mo (モ), u (ウ), se (セ), ya (ヤ), ku (ク), yo (ヨ), te (テ), ka (カ), ro (ロ), so (ソ), ho (ホ), na (ナ), yu (ユ), me (メ), nu (ヌ), ne (ネ), re (レ)

APPENDIX A

The Syllabary

The katakana syllabary charts should read: **a** (ah), i (ēē), u (ōō), e (eh), o (oh); **ka,** ki, ku, ke, ko; **sa,** shi, su, se, so; **ta,** chi, tsu, te, to; **na,** ni, nu, ne, no; **ha,** hi, fu, he, ho; **ma,** mi, mu, me, mo; **ya,** (yi), yu, (ye), yo; **ra,** ri, ru, re, ro; **wa,** n.

Katakana spelling

ア	カ	サ	タ	ナ	ハ	マ	ヤ	ラ	ワ
イ	キ	シ	チ	ニ	ヒ	ミ	ヰ	リ	ン
ウ	ク	ス	ツ	ヌ	フ	ム	ユ	ル	
エ	ケ	セ	テ	ネ	ヘ	メ	エ	レ	
オ	コ	ソ	ト	ノ	ホ	モ	ヨ	ロ	

Roman spelling (rōmaji)

a	ka	sa	ta	na	ha	ma	ya	ra	wa
i	ki	shi	chi	ni	hi	mi	(yi)	ri	n/m
u	ku	su	tsu	nu	fu	mu	yu	ru	
e	ke	se	te	ne	he	me	(ye)	re	
o	ko	so	to	no	ho	mo	yo	ro	

Lesson first introduced

1	2	10	4	8	9	16	18	1	4
3	6	4	7	10	1	8	18	2	2/11
6	4	3	5	17	8	5	17	6	
4	7	7	5	16	10	2	18	3	
5	1	10	3	16	9	16	18	9	

APPENDIX B

Special Symbols, Special Sound Changes

Lesson	Name	Symbol	Sound Change(s)
1	dash	─	lengthens preceding vowel
2	nakaguro	·	separates two-part words
7	small tsu	ッ	doubles following consonant
11	maru	°	changes h and f kanas to p kanas
12	chon-chon	゛	changes h and f kanas to b kanas
13	chon-chon	゛	changes k kanas to g kanas
14	chon-chon	゛	changes t kanas to d kanas (and chi to ji)
15	chon-chon	゛	changes s kanas to z kanas and shi to ji
20	particle	ハ	written ha, pronounced wa
20	particle	ヘ	written he, pronounced e
20	particle	ヲ	written wo, pronounced o

APPENDIX C

Special Kana Combinations

Lesson	Combination	Result(s)	Example
6	u plus small vowel	wi, we, wo	ウィ
8	te plus small i	ti	ティ
9	fu plus small vowel	fa, fi, fe, fo	ファ
14	de plus small i	di	ディ

Lesson	Combination	Result(s)	Example
17	ni, shi, etc. plus small yu	nyu, shu, etc.	ニュ
17	de, fu plus small yu	d(e)yu, f(u)yu	デュ
18	ki, ji, etc. plus small ya	kya, ja, etc.	キャ
18	chi, shi, etc. plus small yo	cho, sho, etc.	チョ
19	chi, shi, ji plus small e	che, she, je	チェ
19	tsu plus small a	tsa	ツァ
19	to, do plus small u	t(o)u, d(o)u	トゥ
19	u plus bu	vu	ヴ
19	vu plus small vowel	va, vi, ve, vo	ヴァ

APPENDIX D

Alternate Roman Spellings

Lesson	This Text	Other Texts	Lesson	This Text	Other Texts
4	ku, k*u*, k'	ku, k'	18	sha	sya, sha
3	su, s*u*, s'	su, s'	17	shu, sh*u*, sh'	syu, shu
5	tsu, ts*u*, ts'	tu, tsu, ts'	18	sho	syo, sho
8	fu, f*u*, f'	hu, fu, f'	15	ji	zi, dzi, di, ji
2	pu, p*u*, p'	pu, p'	18	ja	zya, ja
1	ā	aa, ā	17	ju	zyu, ju
3	ii	ī, ii	18	jo	zyo, jo
6	ū	uu, ū	7	chi	ti, chi, ch'
4	ē, ei	ee, ei, ē	18	cha	tya, cha
5	ō	oo, ou, ō	17	chu	tyu, chu
2	n	ñ, n', n	18	cho	tyo, cho
11	m	ñ, n', n, m	6	u, w	u, w
4	shi	si, shi, sh'	19	b, v	b, v, u

BIBLIOGRAPHY

Akao, Yoshio. *Waei Kihon Tango Jukugo Shū* (Fundamental Japanese-English words & Phrases). Tokyo: Ōbunsha, 1985.

Arakawa, Sōbei. *Kadokawa Gairaigo Jiten* (Kadokawa Loanword Dictionary). 54th edition. Tokyo: Kadokawa Shoten, 1984.

Japan Foundation. *Nihongo Kananyūmon Eigoban* (Nihongo: Kana-An Introduction to the Japanese Syllabary). 2nd edition. Tokyo, 1982.

Kenkyusha. *Kenkyusha's New Little Dictionary* (Shin Ritoru Eiwa-Waei Jiten). 5th edition. Tokyo, 1984.

Kobayashi, Tadao. *Gairaigo Katsuyō Shōjiten* (A Practical Guide to Foreign Words in Japanese). Tokyo: Shinozaki Shorin, 1982.

Martin, Samuel E. *Basic Japanese Conversation Dictionary.* 41st edition. Tokyo: Charles E. Tuttle Company, Inc., 1978.

Miura, Akira. *English Loanwords in Japanese.* Tokyo: Charles E. Tuttle Company, Inc. , 1979.

Richter, E. A. , and Hosokawa, Senjirō. *Machigai darake no Nihon-Eigo* (Common Japanese Errors in English). 13th edition. Tokyo: Eichōsha, 1975.

Sanseidō. *Konsaisu Gairaigo Jiten* (Concise Loanword Dictionary). 3rd edition. Tokyo, 1979.

Yohan Publications, Inc. *Yohan English-Japanese Japanese-English Dictionary.* 6th. edition. Tokyo, 1985.

FOREIGN LANGUAGE BOOKS AND MATERIALS

Spanish
Vox Spanish and English Dictionaries
Cervantes-Walls Spanish and English Dictionary
NTC's Dictionary of Spanish False Cognates
Complete Handbook of Spanish Verbs
Guide to Spanish Suffixes
Nice 'n Easy Spanish Grammar
Spanish Verbs and Essentials of Grammar
Spanish Verb Drills
Getting Started in Spanish
Guide to Spanish Idioms
Guide to Correspondence in Spanish
Diccionario Básico Norteamericano
Diccionario del Español Chicano
Basic Spanish Conversation
Let's Learn Spanish Picture Dictionary
My First Spanish and English Dictionary
Spanish Picture Dictionary
Welcome to Spain
Spanish for Beginners
Spanish à la Cartoon
El alfabeto
Let's Sing and Learn in Spanish
Let's Learn Spanish Coloring Book
Let's Learn Spanish Coloring Book-Audiocassette Package
My World in Spanish Coloring Book
Easy Spanish Word Games and Puzzles
Easy Spanish Crossword Puzzles
Easy Spanish Vocabulary Puzzles
Easy Spanish Word Power Games
How to Pronounce Spanish Correctly

French
NTC's New College French and English Dictionary
NTC's Dictionary of Faux Amis
NTC's Dictionary of Canadian French
French Verbs and Essentials of Grammar
Real French
Getting Started in French
Guide to French Idioms
Guide to Correspondence in French
Nice 'n Easy French Grammar
French à la Cartoon
French for Beginners
Let's Learn French Picture Dictionary
French Picture Dictionary
Welcome to France
The French-Speaking World
L'alphabet
Let's Learn French Coloring Book
Let's Learn French Coloring Book-Audiocassette Package
My World in French Coloring Book
French Verb Drills
Easy French Crossword Puzzles
Easy French Vocabulary Games
Easy French Grammar Puzzles
Easy French Word Games
Easy French Culture Games
How to Pronounce French Correctly
L'Express: Ainsi va la France
L'Express: Aujourd'hui la France
Le Nouvel Observateur: Arts, idées, spectacles
Au courant: Expressions for Communicating in
 Everyday French

Audio and Video Language Programs
Just Listen 'n Learn: Spanish, French, Italian,
 German, Greek, and Arabic
Just Listen 'n Learn PLUS: Spanish, French,
 and German
Conversational...in 7 Days: Spanish, French,
 German, Italian, Rusian, Greek, Portuguese
Practice & Improve Your...Spanish, French,
 German, and Italian
Practice & Improve Your...Spanish, French,
 German, and Italian PLUS
Improve Your...Spanish, French,
 German, and Italian: The P&I Method
VideoPassport French and Spanish

German
Schöffler-Weis German and English Dictionary
Klett German and English Dictionary
Das Max und Moritz Buch
NTC's Dictionary of German False Cognates
Getting Started in German
German Verbs and Essentials of Grammar
Guide to German Idioms
Street-wise German
Nice 'n Easy German Grammar
German à la Cartoon
Let's Learn German Picture Dictionary
German Picture Dictionary
German for Beginners
German Verb Drills
Easy German Crossword Puzzles
Easy German Word Games and Puzzles
Let's Learn German Coloring Book
Let's Learn German Coloring Book-Audiocassette Package
My World in German Coloring Book
How to Pronounce German Correctly
Der Spiegel: Aktuelle Themen in der
 Bundesrepublik Deutschland

Italian
Zanichelli Super-Mini Italian and Dictionary
Zanichelli New College Italian and English Dictionary
Basic Italian Conversation
Getting Started in Italian
Italian Verbs and Essentials of Grammar
Let's Learn Italian Picture Dictionary
My World in Italian Coloring Book
Let's Learn Italian Coloring Book
Let's Learn Italian Coloring Book-Audiocassette Package
How to Pronounce Italian Correctly

Greek and Latin
NTC's New College Greek and English Dictionary
Essentials of Latin Grammar

Russian
Complete Handbook of Russian Verbs
Basic Structure Practice in Russian
Essentials of Russian Grammar
Business Russian
Roots of the Russian Language
Inspector General
Reading and Translating Contemporary Russian
How to Pronounce Russian

Polish
The Wiedza Powszechna Compact Polish and English
 Dictionary

Hebrew
Everyday Hebrew

Japanese
101 Japanese Idioms
Japanese in Plain English
Everyday Japanese
Japanese for Children
Japan Today!
Easy Hiragana
Easy Katakana
Easy Kana Workbook
How to Pronounce Japanese Correctly

Korean
Korean in Plain English

Chinese
Easy Chinese Phrasebook and Dictionary
Basic Chinese Vocabulary

Swedish
Swedish Verbs and Essentials of Grammar

Ticket to...Series
France, Germany, Spain, Italy (Guidebook and
 Audiocassette)

"Just Enough" Phrase Books
Chinese, Dutch, French, German, Greek, Hebrew,
 Hungarian, Italian, Japanese, Portuguese, Russian,
 Scandinavian, Serbo-Croat, Spanish
Business French, Business German, Business Spanish

PASSPORT BOOKS
a division of NTC Publishing Group
Lincolnwood, Illinois USA